IN MEXICO

REVISED EDITION

Antony Keble
Tim Connell

Language consultants
Alberto Palaus
Juanita Garciagodoy

EMC/Paradigm Publishing, Saint Paul, Minnesota

About this book

In Mexico enables students to get to know the United States' southern neighbor—its past and present. The book is full of the type of cultural background information essential to any student of New World Spanish. Communicative language is presented in context to help students cope with everyday situations, whether they are learning Spanish in the classroom or on a visit to Mexico. Wherever possible, authentic material is included to bring Mexico and its language to life.

For easy reference the book is divided into three sections:
Before you go gives background information on Mexican history, culture, food and family life. It also provides helpful trip-planning tips.
In Mexico is a practical guide for visitors to the country, including the following: places to see, how to travel around, going shopping, entertainment suggestions, writing or calling home. There is a quick quiz (page 62) so students can find out how much they have discovered about Mexico from the book.
Central and South America takes a look at the other Spanish-speaking countries of Latin America. It gives an outline of their geography, history and key points of interest, reflecting the diversity of the many Spanish-speaking countries of Latin America.

In the book look out for:

¿Cómo se dice?: gives key vocabulary and phrases for different situations, like making a phone call or ordering a meal in a restaurant.

¿Sabes que...?: highlights information on interesting or unusual subjects.

¡Mira!: indicates points or places of interest in Mexico.

Here are some points to help students and teachers:
- In the book, the names of people and places usually appear in their Spanish form, even in the English text. Mexico, Panama and Peru are exceptions; they appear without accents.
- Spanish words in the middle of English text are in bold type. The first time they appear, they are usually followed by an explanation in English, except where the meaning is clear from the context.
- In Mexican Spanish, the word **futbol** appears without an accent; in other parts of Latin American it has an accent—**fútbol**. In this book, it appears without an accent, as in Mexico.
- The meaning of a word may vary from country to country. The usual meaning of **el coco** is 'coconut' or 'coconut palm'. In Colombia and Ecuador, it also means 'derby hat'! Sometimes, different words are used to describe the same thing. For Mexicans an avocado is **un aguacate**, while in Peru and Bolivia it is called **una palta**.
- Although the formal grammar of New World Spanish is much the same in all the Spanish-speaking countries, the way the language is pronounced differs slightly. A native speaker of Spanish can tell whether a person comes from Mexico or Chile, Argentina or Cuba.
- In many Latin American countries, people may say, «**¿Habla castellano?**» when they mean «**¿Habla español?**». Originally, **castellano** was the dialect spoken by people from Castile in central Spain, but now it is often used to describe the Spanish language.
- When you first meet someone, it is best to address them as **usted**. As you get to know people better, you can say **tú**. In New World Spanish, **ustedes** is used as a plural for **tú** and **usted**. (In Spain, **vosotros** (plural) is used for people you know well, and **ustedes** (plural) is the polite form.)
- When you meet or are introduced to people in Latin America, it is usual to shake hands and say **Buenos días**, **Buenas tardes**, or **Buenas noches**, depending on the time of day.

ISBN 0-8219-1260-7
Catalog No. 70348
Published by
EMC/Paradigm Publishing
875 Montreal Way
Saint Paul,
Minnesota 55102, USA

Produced by
Chancerel International Publishers Ltd.
120 Long Acre, London WC2E 9PA

Printed in Hong Kong

Acknowledgements
Aeroméxico; Annuncios en directorios; Aripo; Autobuses de Oriente; Bancomer; Benitos; Patricia Bickford de la Cerda; Barbara Comber; CBS/Columbia Mexico; Corporación Estatal Petrolera Ecuatoriana; CODELCO-Chile; Corporación de Turismo de Venezuela (CORPOTURISMO); Cromos; Denny's; Departamento de Turismo, Gobierno de Jalisco; Dirección del COPLADE-DF, Mexico City; Departamento de Industria, Turismo e Integración, Peru; Elektra Records; El Tapatío; Embajada de Bolivia; Embajada de Brasil; Embajada de Ecuador; Embajada de Uruguay; Embajada de Venezuela; Ferrocarriles Nacionales de México; Florería Clavelito; Focolare; Hotel Ambassador; Hotel El Mirador; Hotel Lastra; Hotel Terranova; Hoteles Canada; Hoteles Nueva Galicia; Instituto Allende; Instituto Boliviano de Turismo; LADECO (Linea Aérea del Cobre) S.A.; Liverpool; Mexican Government Tourist Office; Mexicana de Avación; Pemex; Revista Teleguía; Sangay; Sonodisc; Televisa; Zapata; Video Arte 2000

CONTENTS

	In Mexico	Workbook

Photographs
Neg. 286846, courtesy of Department Library Services, American Museum of Natural History 8; Ancient Arch and Architecture Collection 68; Andes Press Agency 19; A-Z Botanical Collection 9 (2), 47, 74; Bodleian Library 16; B. Box 25; British Museum, London 69; British Museum, London/Bridgeman Art Library 7; British Petroleum 75; P. Cassidy 5(3), 41, 45 (5), 58; Chancerel Publishers Ltd. 23; J. Chipps 12 (2), 13, 62 (2); Codelco-Chile 75; Das Photo/D. Simson 4, 5 (3), 6 (3), 7, 10 (2), 11 (2), 14, 15, 17 (2), 18 (3), 20 (2), 21 (3), 22, 24 (2), 26 (2), 27, 38, 31 (3), 32 (6), 33, 34 (2), 35 (2), 36 (6), 37 (4), 38, 41 (5), 42 (2), 43, 44, 45 (6), 47, 50 (3), 52 (3), 53, 54 (2), 55 (2), 56, 57 (2), 58 (2), 59 (2), 60 (2), 61, 63 (7), 72, 73, 74; Enciclopedia de México 9, 13, 14, 15, 17; Mary Evans Picture Library 10, 70, 71; M. Fini 73 (2), 79; S. Fraser 5, 64; Fyffes 74; Mary Glasgow Publications Ltd. 15, 17; B. Hallmann 4; D. Horwell 65, 65, 67; A. Keble 6 (2), 7, 10, 12 (2), 13 (2), 17, 18, 23, 24, 25, 26 (4), 39 (3), 32 (2), 34, 36 (2), 37 (2), 38, 40, 41, 44, 46 (20, 49, 50, 51 (2), 52, 57, 58, 59, 61 (2); Liverpool 42 (5), 43 (3); Mansell Collection 69, 70, 71; Mexican Ministry of Tourism 6, 7, 9, 15, 16 (2), 17, 20 (2), 30, 31, 35 (2), 43, 44, 45, 46 (3), 47 (2), 49 (3), 50 (5), 54, 55; Multivision 11; National Gallery 11; Nolper Asociados 49; Pemex 15; Bob Reeve Collection/Reeve Aleutian Airways Inc. 67; South American Pictures 64, 76; Sporting Pictures 56, 79; St. Augustine and St. Johns Chamber of Commerce 9.

Front cover: South American Pictures
Back cover: Top left: Codex Mendoza (Bodleian Library); top right: Mexico City (Das Photo/D. Simson).

Every effort has been made to contact the copyright holders of all illustrations. The publishers apologize for any omissions and will be pleased to make the necessary arrangements at the first opportunity.

Bienvenidos a México

!Hola¡ ¡Muy bienvenidos! Me llamo Ana. I'm going to tell you about Mexico where I live—and other Spanish-speaking countries in Latin America. Look at this map to see where people speak Spanish.

Hi! My name is James. I'm studying Spanish at school and I'm going to Mexico next vacation. I can hardly wait!

Canadá

Estados Unidos

México

Cuba

Belice

Jamaica

Haití

Puerto Rico

República Dominicana

Guatemala

Honduras

El Salvador

Nicaragua

Costa Rica

Panamá

Venezuela

Colombia

Ecuador

Brasil

Perú

Bolivia

Paraguay

Chile

Argentina

Uruguay

¿Sabes que . . . ?

★ Approximately 316 million people in the world speak Spanish as their first language.

★ In the largest country in South America, Brazil, they speak Portuguese not Spanish. In 1493, Pope Alexander VI settled a dispute between Spain and Portugal by drawing a line down the Atlantic Ocean. The arrangement gave most of the Americas to the Spanish, leaving only Brazil for the Portuguese.

Except for the accents, most of the names on the map look almost the same in Spanish as in English. Try saying them the Spanish way. Is there a big difference?

English words are sometimes used in Spanish, but they are written differently so that they can be pronounced easily by Spanish-speaking people. What are these English words?

El líder

El coctel

El dólar

El champú

El béisbol

El nocaut

Do try:
□ to speak as much Spanish as possible. Nobody cares if you make a mistake, but people will appreciate your trying.
□ to learn new words from what you see and hear.
□ to guess the meaning of a word you don't know from the meaning of the words around it.
□ to watch for things that are new and interesting.

donde el castellano es la/una lengua oficial

y a la América Latina

What's there to see?

La costa

Playa del Carmen, México

El río Napo, Ecuador

La selva

El desierto

Las líneas de Nazca, Perú

La montaña

El volcán Aconcagua, Argentina

La gente

Un mexicano

Una mexicana

Los monumentos históricos

Las ruinas de Tikal, Guatemala

Los campesinos de Tarabuco, Bolivia

¿Sabes que...?

★ There are 732 million Americans...
  - 302 million in South America
  - 430 million in North America (including Central American countries, the Caribbean, Mexico, USA and Canada).

Pre-Columbian civilizations

Christopher Columbus was aiming for the East Indies when he arrived in what is now called the Americas, so he called the people there 'Indians'. Nowadays, the civilizations that existed before Columbus arrived are known as pre-Columbian.

From Olmecs to Aztecs

1500 BC

The most ancient advanced culture is that of the Olmecs, who appeared around 1500 BC in southeastern Mexico. They later built a large ceremonial site at La Venta near the Gulf Coast, as well as 10-foot high stone heads, weighing up to 20 tons. They had a calendar and an early form of writing.

AD 100

The Mayan empire extended from what is today Guatemala and Honduras into the Yucatán. The Mayas developed Olmec astronomy and mathematics and were noted for their massive stone temples, sculpture, pottery and textiles. They built the magnificent religious centers of Palenque and Uxmal (Mexico) and Tikal (Guatemala). Later, under Toltec influence, Chichén Itzá was constructed.

Una cabeza gigante olmeca

La pirámide del Sol, Teotihuacán

Una pirámide maya, Uxmal

At its peak, Teotihuacán, near present-day Mexico City, had several thousand inhabitants. It was overrun in AD 750, but the giant Pyramids of the Sun and the Moon can still be seen, as can the 'Street of the Dead,' a wide avenue linking several plazas. Murals were painted inside temples and ordinary houses. One depicts the watery paradise of the rain god, Tlaloc.

For a thousand years up to AD 1000 the Zapotecs took over the sacred mountaintop site of Monte Albán in Oaxaca. Many of the temples and pyramids there date from the eighth century. Excavation of tombs, cut into the rock, revealed jewelry and metal objects buried with the bodies.

El sitio de Monte Albán ▶

AD 900

In the tenth century, the Toltecs made their capital at Tula and gained control of the central part of Mexico. Quetzalcóatl, the feathered snake, was one of their main gods. Toltec culture influenced the Aztecs. Eventually civil war pushed the Toltecs down into the Yucatán, the land of the Mayas.

AD 1300

The Aztecs or Mexicas appeared late in Mexican history as a tribe which migrated to central Mexico in the 13th century. Their priests told them to build their city where they found an eagle with a snake in its beak and perched on a cactus. In 1325, the city of Tenochtitlán was founded on two islands in Lake Texcoco. The Aztecs fought and took control of the surrounding tribes, from whom they demanded sacrificial victims, gold, food and exotic birds and animals.

When the Spaniards arrived, Tenochtitlán was a magnificent city of canals, temples, houses with roof gardens and a great marketplace, linked to the lakeshore by three causeways.

- How did Mexico get its name?

Columnas en forma de guerreros, Tula

La ciudad de Tenochtitlán

Life before the Conquest

Comprando tortillas en el mercado

Daily life was organized around the community, and the individual had little independence. The annual food-growing cycle was broken by religious festivals which were occasions for dancing, feasts and music.

Land was held by the tribe as a whole and families were allocated plots to grow food on. The ground was prepared for planting with a pointed stick—there were no ploughs. There were no horses, cows, pigs, sheep or goats either.

People were mainly vegetarian, eating a basic diet of **tortillas** (cornmeal bread), beans and chilies, which has remained the same for thousands of years. Sometimes they also had turkey or fish.

The wheel was only used on children's toys. Any goods to be transported from one place to another were taken by canoe or carried by porters.

Ordinary houses were built of wood or **adobe** (sun-dried mud) with thatched roofs. Skilled architects, mathematicians and stone carvers built enormous, elaborate temples and palaces. Copper, lead, tin, silver and gold (but not iron) were mined and worked. Craftsmen made little statues and jewelry from jade, gold and silver. The women wove cotton cloth into geometric or flower patterns. There was pottery in the shape of human figures, plants and animals.

● The words for two food products come from the Mexican Indian words, **xocóatl** and **tomátl**. What are their English names?

The last Aztec emperors

Moctezuma was emperor of the Aztecs when the Spanish came. He had absolute power over his people, but he still had to obey the wishes of the gods. There had been omens. Shooting stars were thought to foretell the return of the god Quetzalcóatl and the destruction of the Aztec cities. When a small Spanish army landed at the coast and reports of these white-skinned men with fair beards came to Tenochtitlán, Moctezuma was undecided. Instead of resisting, he let the Spanish into the city. He was later killed by his own people, who felt he had betrayed them.

The last Aztec emperor was Moctezuma's nephew, Cuauhtémoc. When the Spanish attacked Tenochtitlán in 1521, Cuauhtémoc resisted for 75 days in a terrible battle during which thousands of Aztecs died. Eventually, he was captured and later hanged in 1525.

● The Aztec version of Moctezuma is Motecuhzoma, but the Spaniards found it difficult to say and pronounced it Moctezuma. Do you know what he is called in English?

The pre-Columbian gods usually represented the forces of nature, like the sun, the moon, the earth or thunder, or were identified with a particular tribe. They were shown as part human, part animal, or as a combination of different animals, like the snake and jaguar. Religion had an important place in the life of the people, as it explained things they didn't understand. From their observations of the stars, the priests developed calendars which they used to tell people when to plant and harvest crops.

¿Sabes que . . . ?

★ There are over 14,000 archeological sites in Mexico.

Quetzalcóatl, one of the gods worshiped by the Toltecs and later the Aztecs. The name means 'bird snake'. When a 10th-century Toltec priest-king, who had fair hair and a beard, took the same name, history and myth were mingled. Legend said that, in the form of a white-skinned, fair-bearded man, Quetzalcóatl had gone to the sea in the east, but would one day return. When the Spanish landed on the eastern coast of Mexico in 1519, the Aztecs were not sure whether they were gods or men.

Exploring a New World

La Conquista

After Columbus, the Spanish began to explore the 'New World' they had arrived in. They settled in the Caribbean, on Hispaniola (the island now divided into the Dominican Republic and Haiti), Cuba and Puerto Rico. From there, expeditions set out for what is now North, Central and South America.

In defiance of the governor of Cuba, Hernán Cortés sailed to explore the Gulf of Mexico in 1519. He landed near the site of the modern city of Veracruz. He had only a few hundred men, but they had horses and guns which the local people had never seen before. At first, they thought that a horse and its rider were one terrifying creature!

Cortés formed an alliance with the people of the coast, who hated the Aztecs, and boldly rode to the Aztec capital, Tenochtitlán. There he met the Aztec emperor, Moctezuma, and later took him hostage.

Soldiers from Cuba were sent to arrest Cortés, so he returned to the coast. Cortés persuaded the soldiers sent to arrest him that they would do better to join him and share the glory of conquering a new territory for Spain — as well as the Aztec treasure.

In Tenochtitlán, the Spanish in panic massacred a large number of Aztecs at a religious festival. When Cortés returned, he found chaos. He had Moctezuma dragged to a roof top and ordered him to tell his people to let the Spanish leave. The answer was a shower of stones which killed Moctezuma. The people later attacked Cortés and his soldiers. The next night the Spanish retreated along

Cuauhtémoc is shown surrendering to Cortés. Today there are many memorials to Cuauhtémoc, but few to Cortés. Since Mexico gained independence from Spain more than 150 years ago, people have come to appreciate their pre-Columbian heritage much more.

the causeway across the lake, carrying the gold that they had looted. So many Spanish were killed that the night was called **la noche triste** (the sad night). Cortés rallied his soldiers and, in the following months, attacked again. Finally in 1521, the Spanish took control of the city of Tenochtitlán and captured the emperor, Cuauhtémoc.

For God and gold

The Spanish who went to the 'New World' of the Americas were authorized by the Pope to convert the local people to Christianity. There were also many battle-hardened soldiers in Spain who had spent years fighting to drive the Moors from Spain. After the fighting ended, these soldiers went to look for adventure in the 'New World'.

Hernán Cortés went to Mexico in search of gold. He told the Aztec emperor, Moctezuma, "The Spanish have a disease that can only be cured by gold." When he and his men arrived in Tenochtitlán, they were amazed to see so much gold and silver in the city. After the Conquest, all the mines belonged to the king of Spain. The local people, who mined the gold and silver, worked deep underground and thousands died of disease, hunger and overwork.

During the Conquest, local temples were destroyed and Christian churches were often built on the sites of these temples. Elements of the new and the old religions sometimes became intermingled. Thousands of people were baptized, some by force.

Many of the early Christian missionaries learned how to speak the local languages. With the help of the Aztecs, one priest, Fray Bernardino de Sahagún, collected invaluable information about history, laws, customs, religion and the arts for his ***Historia General de las Cosas de Nueva España***.

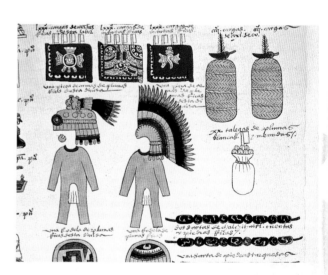

The Codex Mendoza, an illustrated manuscript, was commissioned by Antonio de Mendoza, the first viceroy of Spain's new lands in the Americas. The items shown were given as tributes to the Spanish and include woven cloth (top left), chilies (top right) and feathered headdresses.

The people of New Spain

After the Conquest the Indians were often treated like slaves. Many were forced to work on the lands given to **los conquistadores**, the Spanish soldiers who had conquered their country.

Soon there were many children of mixed parentage (Indian and Spanish), called **mestizos**. They came to despise their own Indian ancestry and looked down on those who were of pure Indian origin.

Mexico was a colony of Spain from 1519 to 1821 and many Spanish people settled there. The descendants of the original Spaniards became known as **criollos**. Through strict intermarriage with other **criollos**, they maintained control of the **haciendas** (plantations) and **ranchos** (cattle farms) from generation to generation. **Mestizos** and Indians provided the labor.

The administrators and merchants who came from Spain later in the colonial period were known as **peninsulares**, because Spain lies on a peninsula. They considered themselves superior to the **criollos**.

Mexico itself was only one part of **Nueva España** (New Spain), which also included Central America and the Spanish Caribbean islands. **El virrey** (the viceroy) ruled the colony on behalf of **el rey** (the king of Spain). The **virreyes** were usually Spanish noblemen who never intended to make Mexico their home. They stayed for some years and returned to Spain.

The original building of the González-Alvarez house in St. Augustine, Florida, was constructed in the early 1600s. It was later rebuilt in 1702 after the town was burned by English troops fighting against the Spanish and is one of the oldest Spanish houses in the USA.

*A rigid social system developed. At the top were the **virrey** and the **peninsulares** who ran the country; next came the **criollos**, then the **mestizos** and various classes down to the Indians, who were poor and often slaves.*

Many new foods and products, like corn, tobacco, tomatoes and chocolate, were taken from Mexico to Spain. Horses, sheep, cows, pigs, wheat, olives and grapes came from Spain. Trade with English-speaking territories further north was forbidden, because Spain wanted to keep Mexico as a market for its own exports.

When the Mexican vineyards started to produce enough wine to supply local needs, they were forced to uproot their vines because Spanish winemakers feared the competition. After that, wine had to come thousands of miles from Spain and was very expensive.

*One of the best of the 61 **virreyes** who ruled Mexico was the first— Antonio de Mendoza. Appointed in 1535 by the Spanish king, he helped develop education and the economy of the new colony. He also organized an expedition, led by Francisco Vásquez de Coronado, which explored north as far as present-day Kansas and claimed all the territories in between for the crown of Spain.*

¿Sabes que . . .?

★ No one is sure how many Indians were living in Mexico when the Spanish came. Estimates vary from three to 20 million! But at least half the Indian population died of diseases—smallpox, typhus, cholera—brought by the Spanish. As these illnesses had not existed in their country before the Conquest, the Indians had no natural resistance—even the flu could kill them.

9

¡Viva la independencia!

The movement towards independence

In 1808 the French Emperor Napoleon invaded Spain and took Carlos IV prisoner. Carlos had to give up his throne to Napoleon's brother, Joseph.

The rich, landowning **criollos** in Mexico felt no loyalty to a king from France. Inspired by the French Revolution and the American War of Independence, many of them began to think of independence for their own country. Some Mexicans even fought with the Americans against the British.

José María Morelos is portrayed sword in hand in a mural by Juan O'Gorman.

A statue of Father Hidalgo, known as **el padre de la patria,** *shown breaking the symbolic chains that bound Mexico to the Spanish empire. How would you say* **el padre de la patria** *in English?*

The first man to call openly for revolt was Father Miguel Hidalgo in September, 1810. From his pulpit he demanded freedom for slaves and the redistribution of land in the countryside.

At first he had some success, but his thousands of followers were more of a mob than an organized force. On July 15, 1811, his forces were defeated by a royalist army. Father Hidalgo was taken prisoner and executed by firing squad. His idealism and courage inspired others to fight on.

When Father Hidalgo rebelled, José María Morelos, also a priest, used guerrilla tactics to fight against Spanish control of Mexico. For a time he took over southern Mexico, but was captured by the royalists and shot. One of his recruits, Vicente Guerrero, continued the guerrilla struggle.

Agustín de Iturbide fought on both sides! He was an officer in the royalist army sent out against Vicente Guerrero. Later, he changed sides and joined Guerrero. In 1821, Iturbide led the rebel army in the overthrow of Spanish power, and Mexico gained independence.

In the confusion following independence, Iturbide had himself crowned Emperor of Mexico in May, 1822. Ten months later he was overthrown by General Santa Anna, and the Mexican congress chose Guadalupe Victoria as president.

Agustín de Iturbide shown in an extract from a picture history of Mexico. Why was he considered the most suitable person to negotiate with the rebels?

Presidents and dictators

The first president of Mexico was ex-guerrilla leader Guadalupe Victoria (1824–29). During these years, the liberal **mestizos** *struggled for power with the conservative* **criollos***.*

General Antonio López de Santa Anna was in and out of power nine times. When Mexico banned slavery in its territory, Texas, in 1835, Texas declared itself independent. In his efforts to recover Texas, Santa Anna won the Battle of the Alamo, but was defeated and captured at the Battle of San Jacinto.

In 1846, border incidents led to the Mexican War. Santa Anna led Mexico's resistance to American forces, but Mexico City was occupied in 1847 and Santa Anna surrendered. Under the Treaty of Guadalupe Hidalgo, signed February 2, 1848, Mexico lost Texas, California, Arizona, Colorado, Nevada, Utah and most of New Mexico—half its national territory.

- *What do you think New Mexico's original name was in Spanish?*
- *The US states of Montana, California, Colorado, Nevada and Florida were all named by the Spanish. Find out what the names mean.*

Shown here in a Juan O'Gorman mural in the Palacio Nacional, Mexico City, is Benito Juárez. One of Mexico's most able leaders, he was president four times between 1858 and 1872. Born to a poor Zapotec Indian family in Oaxaca, he only began to learn Spanish at the age of 12. He first studied to be a priest, but was later drawn to law. By the age of 42 he had become governor of his home state. He governed Oaxaca so well that it became a model for other Mexican states. His honesty and hard work made him a popular governor and president.

*In the War of Reform (1858–1860), Juárez reflected the hopes of the **mestizos** and the Indians. He spearheaded the resistance to Maximilian. After the retreat of the French, he served two more terms and died in office in 1872.*

Porfirio Díaz was president and virtual dictator of Mexico from 1872 to 1910. He censored the press and favored the Catholic Church. He justified his dictatorship on the grounds that it kept the country stable. Mexico was run as a business, the upper and middle classes and foreign investors prospered, while the majority of the population—the urban and rural poor—suffered.

*Less than one percent of the population owned two-thirds of the land. One family in Chihuahua owned an area larger than the state of Ohio. Those without land worked on the **haciendas**. They had to buy their food and supplies from **tiendas de raya**, where they were often charged twice the regular price, and quickly ran up debts. If they tried to run away they were tracked down by the **rurales**, the cruel country police.*

In mines and factories, working conditions were also appalling. After 38 years, the people's resentment found expression in the Revolution of 1910.

The Revolution of 1910

The Revolution started in the north. Demands for free elections came from Francisco Madero, a landowner from Coahuila. He gained the support of northern landowners and **vaqueros** (cowboys) who had no sympathy for the central government. Among them was cowboy turned bandit and guerrilla leader Pancho (Francisco) Villa. In the south, a peasant leader appeared, Emiliano Zapata. His rallying cry was **Tierra y Libertad**.

Díaz fled to exile in France, and Madero became president. He was an idealist, but not an effective leader. A counter-revolution was started against him by former Díaz supporters. In 1913, the army chief, Victoriano Huerta, changed sides and had Madero murdered, taking power for himself.

Years of bloodshed followed. The head of the opposition to Huerta was Venustiano Carranza, governor of Coahuila, helped by his right-hand man, General Angel Obregón. Their allies were Pancho Villa and Emiliano Zapata. Huerta was driven out and, like Díaz, went into exile in France.

Disagreements between Carranza, Villa and Zapata led to further fighting. Carranza and Villa both wanted to be president. Zapata was principally interested in land reform for the poor.

The combined armies of Villa and Zapata captured Mexico City in December 1914, but were soon defeated. In 1917, a new constitution was drawn up and Carranza was elected president. Zapata was lured into an ambush and murdered in 1919. Villa was assassinated in 1923.

- What does Zapata's slogan **Tierra y Libertad** mean in English?

*Villa (left) trying the presidential chair for size during the 1914 occupation of Mexico City. Zapata (right) has his famous **sombrero** on his knee.*

In January, 1862, four years after Juárez became president, a combined Spanish, English and French army landed in Veracruz, demanding payment of debts owed by Mexico. By April, the English and Spanish had withdrawn, but after a defeat at Puebla, the French army captured Mexico City.

The French emperor, Napoleon III, appointed the Archduke of Austria, Maximilian, as Emperor of Mexico. Maximilian believed that the people of Mexico wanted him. The Mexicans, who had struggled so hard for independence, did not want a foreigner ruling over them and, led by Juárez, fought back.

In 1866, Napoleon III withdrew his army, leaving Maximilian without support. He was captured by Juárez's soldiers and executed by firing squad.

La República de México

México or México?

Mexico is a federal republic of 31 states. Mexicans often say **la República** when they are talking about their country. The official name for Mexico City is **la ciudad de México**, but most people simply call it **México**. It is the capital and is in **un distrito federal**. On Mexican coins is written **Estados Unidos Mexicanos** —the United States of Mexico.

Snra. M. García de Mendoza
Calle 16 de Septiembre 43
Col. Centro
Del. Cuauhtémoc
México, D.F.

POR AVION
AIR MAIL

What does Mexico mean to Mexicans?

This is **la bandera nacional**.

- What does D.F. stand for in this address?
- Name two other countries in the world that have their capital in a federal district.

- Can you describe its colors in Spanish?
- Why is there an eagle with a snake in the middle of the flag?
- What color are the edges of Mexican air mail envelopes? Why are these colours used?

The government

Under the 1917 constitution, the government has an executive section, headed by **el Presidente** (president). **La Cámara de diputados** (equivalent to the House of Representatives) and **el Senado** (Senate) make up the congress.

There is a presidential election every six years. Presidents can only be elected once. **Los diputados** (Representatives) are elected every three years and **los senadores** (senators) every six years.

In Mexico, it is the president who really holds power. As head of the government party, **el Partido Revolucionario Institucional** or **PRI**, he chooses **los diputados** (Representatives) for election and his own successor. In 1994, the President announced that he would change this system to allow greater democracy into the PRI.

The PRI has governed Mexico since 1946. Before that, under different names, it has held power since 1929. It has a wide base of support drawn from the most important labor union, **la Confederación de Trabajadores de México**, which represents a third of the labor force, and from farmers' and professional organizations.

The main opposition parties are **el Partido de Acción Nacional** or **PAN** and **el Partido de Revolución Democrática** or **PRD**.

- What does this PRI slogan say?

¿Quién es?

12

The Catholic Church

As most Mexicans are Catholics, the Catholic Church plays an important part in daily life.

Many of the most beautiful churches date back to colonial times. They were often built on the sites of Aztec temples, using stones from ruined pyramids. Inside the old churches there are often elaborate altars decorated with gold and silver.

This is an altar in San ▶ Agustín, Guanajuato.
- Why do you think so much gold was used to decorate the altar?

- This notice is outside ▶ a church. What must you make sure of before going in?

◀ This is a bulletin board for a Protestant church.
- What happens on Sundays at 10 am?
- When is the office open?

La Virgen de Guadalupe

Every year on December 12, crowds gather at the Basilica of Our Lady of Guadalupe in Mexico City. In every town and village in Mexico there are processions in honor of **Nuestra Señora de Guadalupe**. They commemorate the occasion when, in 1531, the Virgin Mary appeared five times to an Indian convert to Christianity, Juan Diego, and his uncle. She asked that a shrine to her be built on that spot which had been a temple to an Aztec goddess, Tonantzin.

Our Lady of Guadalupe is the patron saint of Mexico. Father Hidalgo adopted a banner of **la Virgen de Guadalupe** when he began the fight for independence. During the 1910 Revolution, Zapata supporters wore pictures of her on their **sombreros**.

Many people come to the basilica to pray every year. As a special mark of respect some even come all the way up the avenue to the basilica on their knees.
- Guadalupe Victoria was the name of the first Mexican president, but it wasn't his real name. Why did he change his name?

A devout worshiper at the **Basilica de Guadalupe**.

El Día de los Muertos

November 2 is **el Día de los Muertos**—the day of the dead. A combination of pre-Columbian and Christian customs, it is a time when all those who have died are remembered.

On the night of November 1 (All Saints' Day), the souls of dead children are supposed to return to earth and on the following night adult souls are awaited.

You might think it's a sad occasion, but it's not. People make altars decorated with flowers, with a photo of a dead member of the family. They prepare food and leave it by the photo. Sometimes they go to the cemeteries with candles and flowers and keep watch all night.

As a reminder that death comes to us all, people give little presents showing death in different forms, a mariachi player or a devil. They also offer each other skulls—not real ones, they're made of sugar and decorated with pink and blue icing.
- Do we have a festival that is celebrated around the same time as **el Día de los Muertos**? How did it originate? How do we celebrate it?

¡Mira!

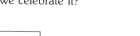

☞ Look for pictures of Our Lady of Guadalupe in Mexico.
☞ If you're in Mexico for **el Día de los Muertos**, how many death figures can you see?

At work

Working in the city

¿Dónde viven y trabajan los mexicanos? ¡Mira el mapa!

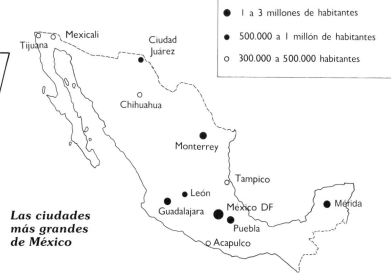

●	20 millones de habitantes
●	1 a 3 millones de habitantes
●	500.000 a 1 millón de habitantes
○	300.000 a 500.000 habitantes

Las ciudades más grandes de México

In the last 20 years the number of people living in Mexico City has doubled, making it one of the fastest growing cities in the world. It is estimated that by the year 2010 one third of Mexicans will live in and around the capital, which already has about 20 million people.

Many people come to Mexico City after abandoning the harsh life of peasant farming. They come to search for jobs in the capital which accounts for over half of Mexico's industrial production.

The fast growth of Mexico City has caused problems like housing shortages, strain on public utilities and some of the world's worst traffic jams. Atmospheric pollution reaches very high levels, although the relocation of some major industries has helped to reduce the level of lead and sulfur emissions. The Mexico City newspapers give air-quality reports every day.

● Look at the map of Mexico above and answer these questions.
  a Where is Mexico City? Is it in the north or the south of the country?
  b Which is the nearest large city to Mexico City?
  c Which is the largest of the cities on the Mexican-US border?
  d Which population category does the city of Mérida in the Yucatán Peninsula come into?

The oil industry

Oil was discovered in Mexico at the end of the last century. The country has some of the largest oil and natural gas reserves in the world and is the sixth largest oil producer.

The oil industry was started by British and American companies. By 1921, Mexico was the world's leading producer. The foreign oil companies made large profits and operated without any control by the Mexican government. This caused resentment among Mexicans. In March 1938, President Lázaro Cárdenas expelled the oil companies and nationalized their operations.

Today, the oil industry is run by the government corporation, **Petróleos Mexicanos**, also known as **Pemex**. Oil is a major export, especially to the United States. In 1987, 40 percent of government revenues came from oil. By 1994, this had declined to 20 percent. This makes the economy vulnerable to price fluctuations in the international oil market.

Aware that eventually oil will run out, Mexico is seeking other energy sources. Hydroelectric plants currently generate 20 percent of electricity.

Two-thirds of oil comes from offshore wells, like the one above, in the Gulf of Mexico, near Veracruz. Most of the onshore wells are in the southeast towards the Guatemalan border in the Chiapas-Tabasco region.

What kind of job . . . ?

Un granjero

Un pescador

Una obrera

Un petrolero

Una profesora

Un minero

Un mesero

Un ingeniero

- Who works in which industry or sector? Match the job with the industry or sector.

El petróleo	**La agricultura**
El turismo	**La enseñanza**
La minería	**La hidroelectricidad**
La pesca	**La industria textil**

Mi padre es vendedor.

Mi madre es abogada.

- Can you say in Spanish what jobs your mother and father do?

The tourist business

The country's second largest source of foreign exchange earnings is an invisible export—tourism. Nearly seven million tourists a year visit Mexico. Many of them come from the US and Canada. The service sector, including tourism, is the largest employer in Mexico, providing jobs for a third of the work force.

Mexico has thousands of miles of coastline washed by the waters of the Pacific Ocean, the Gulf of Mexico and the Caribbean Sea. Tourists come in search of sun during the northern winter. Acapulco, known as **la Riviera de las Américas**, was the main destination for many years, but other Pacific resorts, like Puerto Vallarta and Ixtapa, and Cancún on the Caribbean coast are also popular.

Tourists shopping in Mexico

¿Sabes que . . . ?

★ Mexico is...
  - ☐ the world's largest producer of silver.
  - ☐ the United States' third largest trading partner.
  - ☐ a major exporter of auto parts to the United States.

★ Mexico is among the world's top ten producers of . . .

coffee	sisal
corn	sugar cane
eggs	tomatoes
gasoline	zinc

- What are the Spanish names for these products?

Old and New World artists

History in pictures

Art and literature were blended in the picture writing of the Mayas and Aztecs. These drawings with symbols and decoration were done on bark parchment or deerskin. Known as codices, they recorded legends, stories of gods and kings and the life of the people at the time.

From these drawings we know about the gold and jade jewelry that kings, priests and the aristocracy wore. They also wore brightly-colored feather head-dresses and cloaks. The vivid red and green feathers of the quetzal bird were especially prized.

Special events and scenes from daily life were also depicted in murals or stone carvings on the walls of buildings, like temples and palaces. Small figurines of gods, men and women were made from stone, jade or ceramic. Even everyday items, like drinking cups or jugs, were often designed in the shape of human or animal figures.

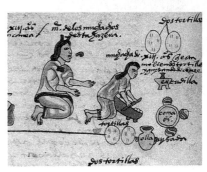

This codex shows a mother teaching her daughter how to grind corn for **tortillas**. The Spaniards wrote in Spanish beside the pictures.
● Why is there a tongue drawn in front of the mother's mouth?
● Why did the Spaniards write on the codices?

Star-gazing

The pre-Columbian peoples, especially the Mayas, were skilled mathematicians and astronomers. They understood the use of zero in mathematics and used their knowledge and observations to chart the position of the sun, moon and stars. They used an 18-month calendar. Each month was divided into 20 days, with five days added to complete the 365-day yearly cycle. This calendar was more accurate than the one used in Europe at the time of Cortés, and existed more than a thousand years before the European Gregorian calendar of 1582, which we still use today.

El calendario azteca en el Museo Nacional de Antropología e Historia de México DF

El observatorio, Chichén Itzá

A woman ahead of her time

One of the most famous literary figures of Mexican colonial times was Sor Juana. Living at a time when many men and women could not even read, Juana Inés de Asbaje y Ramírez de Santillana was brilliant! Born in 1648, she could read by the age of three. As a young girl she learned Latin grammar in 20 lessons!

As she grew up, she was noted for her intelligence, beauty and charm and became a lady-in-waiting at the court of **el virrey**. At the age of 16 she shocked everyone at the court by entering the austere order of Carmelite nuns. She knew that if she married, she would be unlikely to have time to study and write as she wanted. She became known as **Sor** (Sister) Juana Inés de la Cruz.

Sor Juana Inés de la Cruz

She continued her studies in philosophy, mathematics, astronomy and art. Later she joined another order of nuns where life was easier. She wrote plays and prose, but is best remembered for her poetry. One of her most interesting poems is about the mind and what happens to it during sleep.

Shortly before her death, Sor Juana gave away all her possessions, even her beloved books. She died at the age of 47.

Mexican style?

The style of many buildings from the colonial period between 1519 and 1821 is called **el estilo colonial**. Imported from Spain, this architectural style was heavily influenced by pre-Columbian art. Churches, cathedrals and public buildings were constructed, painted and carved by Indians working under Spanish supervision. The Indians learned to paint in a more realistic style, but often kept their own traditional colors and sense of design.

An interesting colonial mansion is **la Casa de los Azulejos** (the House of Tiles) in Mexico City. Built in the 16th century, its rooms overlook a central courtyard called **un patio** (now roofed in). It is decorated, inside and out, with blue and white ceramic tiles.

These architectural features originally came from Moorish North Africa, via Spain.

Since 1903, the building has been a branch of a department-store chain, Sanborns.

During the 17th and 18th centuries, **el barroco**, the baroque style of architecture was popular in Europe. It is characterized by curved lines and very ornate decoration. In Mexico, **el barroco** was developed into something especially Mexican. Many churches were built with domes and every inch of space inside was decorated, often with gilding.

Painters of the Revolution

During the 1920s, a number of artists vividly portrayed the sufferings and ideas of the Revolution of 1910. (Some of them had joined the fighting.) As many people could not read, murals became an imaginative way of illustrating these subjects, and many murals were commissioned for Mexican public buildings.

Modern Mexican murals are an example of how European traditions and the older influences of the Aztec and Mayan frescoes combined to form a style that was uniquely Mexican. Three of the most influential muralists (who also painted on canvas) were Diego Rivera, José Clemente Orozco and David Alfaro Siqueiros.

▲ José Orozco (1883–1949) painted groups of peasants and images of destruction, sacrifice, and rebirth after the Revolution. He experimented with different paints in the search for one that would be weather-resistant when applied directly to concrete.

Man of Fire is painted on the inside of a dome at **el Instituto Cultural Cabañas** in Guadalajara, the city where Orozco was born.

◄ Diego Rivera (1886–1957), who studied under Picasso in Europe, painted Mexican history on a giant scale. One of his murals in **el Palacio Nacional** depicts the fighting during the Conquest.

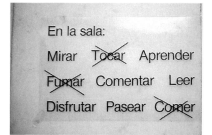

En la sala:

Mirar ~~Tocar~~ Aprender

~~Fumar~~ Comentar Leer

Disfrutar Pasear ~~Comer~~

This is a notice to remind visitors of how they should behave in an art gallery.
- Make a list in English of what you can and can't do.

¡Mira!

☞ How many examples of different architectural styles can you see in Mexico? Take photos or collect postcards of the buildings you see. Write captions for them in Spanish.

☞ Try to see some paintings by Rivera, Orozco, Siqueiros and other famous Mexican painters. What do the paintings show?

☞ Visit a Mexican modern art gallery —you may find some interesting things there!

Money matters

Where do you change money?

La moneda mexicana es el nuevo peso.

Mexican money consists of **el nuevo peso** (new **peso**) which is divided into 100 **centavos** (cents). The symbol for **el nuevo peso** is N$.

Money can be changed at banks, at **casas de cambio** (private exchange offices) and in many hotels. Banks probably give the best rates, but check the **casas de cambio**, too. Hotels generally give the worst rate. Rates vary, even from bank to bank, so it's worth looking around.

Here are a few tips about changing money:

☐ Take most of your money in travelers' checks. Record the numbers and keep them separate and safe. It is also a good idea to have some **pesos** for the day you arrive in Mexico.

☐ Banking hours are normally from 9 am to 1:30 pm, Monday through Friday, but many banks only change money from 9 to midday. **Casas de cambio** are open longer hours. A commission is charged for changing money.

☐ It may be difficult to change money on weekends.

☐ Take your passport with you when changing money.

☐ Many market stalls or shops that deal with tourists may accept American dollars for something you want to buy. But don't expect a very good exchange rate!

CASA DE CAMBIO REFORMA

- Esta casa de cambio está en el centro de la ciudad de México. ¿Cómo se llama la calle dónde está la casa de cambio?

¿Se aceptan tarjetas de crédito en esta tienda?

- How do you say 'credit card' in Spanish? Look at the picture and caption on the left.

¿Cómo se dice?

Buenos días. Quería cambiar dólares en pesos.

¿Es posible cambiar cheques de viajero?

Sí, señor. ¿Cuánto quiere cambiar?

Quería cambiar 20 dólares.

Favor de cobrar en la caja número uno.

CAJA 1

- With a partner, practice changing money in Spanish. One of you is the clerk and the other is a customer changing $75 into **pesos**.

- Practice another dialog for changing money in Spanish. This time one of you wants to change 120 **pesos** into US dollars.

Who's who in pesos

The word **peso** means weight, originally a certain weight of silver. There are **monedas** (coins) of 5, 10, 20, 50 **centavos** and 1, 2, 5 and 10 **nuevos pesos. Los billetes** (bills) are for 10, 20, 50, 100, 200 and 500 **nuevos pesos**. Famous people from Mexican history appear on **los billetes**.

10 nuevos pesos: Emiliano Zapata
20 nuevos pesos: Benito Juárez
50 nuevos pesos: José María Morelos
100 nuevos pesos: Nezahualcóyotl
200 nuevos pesos: Sor Juana
500 nuevos pesos: Ignacio Zaragoza

Nezahuacóyotl (1402-1470), who was ruler of Texcoco, a city-state near Tenochtitlán, also wrote poetry. General Ignacio Zaragoza (1829–1862) helped President Benito Juárez when the French invaded in 1862.

- You can read about the other famous people in this book. See pages 10, 11 and 16. What were the people famous for?

Hay un billete de cien y uno de veinte nuevos pesos.

- Say in Spanish how many **nuevos pesos** pesos are shown in the picture?

Trade and debt crisis

On January 1, 1994, Mexico joined the North American Free Trade Agreement (NAFTA), an economic zone which also includes the United States and Canada. Mexico's membership of NAFTA is expected to build a strong economic interrelationship with these countries.

In 1990, when NAFTA was proposed, Mexico was emerging from the effects of the debt crisis and inflation. The roots of these problems were in the 1970s, when the price of oil was high and Mexico borrowed large sums of money, mainly in American dollars, for development projects.

With the recession in the early 1980s, the oil price fell and so did the peso's value against the dollar. The cost of buying dollars to make the debt repayments rose so much that just paying the interest on the debt caused severe economic hardship. While Mexico honored its debts, life for ordinary Mexicans became very difficult because prices increased so much.

Between 1986 and 1991, inflation averaged 56 percent a year, but, by 1993, it had been reduced to single figures. This was when **el nuevo peso** was introduced.

In the north of Mexico, near the Mexican-US border, there are about 2,000 **maquiladoras**. These are companies which temporarily import raw materials and components duty-free for manufacture or assembly into finished goods. The end product must be exported. More than 500,000 people work in **maquiladoras**.

Planning your trip

> México es un país precioso. Hay muchas regiones distintas.

Noroeste

Estados: Baja California Norte, Baja California Sur, Sonora, Chihuahua, Durango, Sinaloa

This part of the country has dramatic scenery: mostly dry desert and mountains. It's often been used as a setting for cowboy films. **La Sierra Madre Occidental**, the mountain range that runs down the west side of Mexico, starts in the state of Sonora.

The coast along the Gulf of California is greener and used for farming. Rugged mountains also run north-south down the California peninsula. The towns of La Paz and Cabo San Lucas are famous for sport fishing.

Oeste

Estados: Nayarit, Jalisco, Aguascalientes, Guanajuato, Colima, Michoacán

This is an important agricultural area which produces tropical fruit. Tequila, the famous Mexican liquor, comes from a town of the same name in the state of Jalisco. It is made from the leaves of the agave plant.

Mexico's second city, Guadalajara, and nearby Lake Chapala (the country's largest lake) are both in Jalisco. Drawn by the area's beauty, the largest US retirement community in Mexico developed near the lake.

In Morelia, Michoacán's state capital, is **la Universidad de San Nicolás**, founded in 1540. It is one of the oldest universities in the Americas. This part of the country is famous for its good climate. Millions of Monarch butterflies migrate from Canada and the northern US to spend the winter near Zicuaro, Michoacán.

In the state capitals of Aguascalientes, Zacatecas, Guanajuato and Morelia are many fine colonial buildings. Along this coast are several resorts, among them Puerto Vallarta and Manzanillo.

Nordeste

Estados: Coahuila, Nuevo León, Tamaulipas, San Luis Potosí, Zacatecas

Towards the Gulf of Mexico the desert of the northern states gives way to forests and lakes. Tamaulipas is famous for its hunting and fishing, while Coahuila is Mexico's main wine-producing state. Monterrey, capital of Nuevo León, is an industrial center and the third largest city in the country. Many fine buildings from the colonial period can be seen in the towns of Zacatecas, Saltillo and San Luis Potosí.

¿Sabes que . . . ?

★ The 24-hour clock is used in Mexico, especially for official timings, like air or train schedules. For example, 8 o'clock at night is **veinte horas (20h)**.
What time is:
– **trece horas?**
– **23h?**

La costa de Baja California

Las montañas desiertas de Chihuahua

Las mariposas de Zicuaro, Michoacán

El lago de Chapala, Jalisco

Sur

Estados: Morelos, Guerrero, Oaxaca

The state of Guerrero has jungle-covered mountains and beautiful beaches, including the world-famous resort of Acapulco. The thick jungles extend into the state of Oaxaca and support a variety of wildlife. The area is rich in Indian lore and history, too, with the archeological sites of Monte Albán and Mitla. State capital Oaxaca has elegant buildings from its colonial past.

El puerto de Veracruz

Este

Estados: Puebla, Tlaxcala, Veracruz

The states of Puebla and Tlaxcala are on the edge of the central plateau. Although Veracruz is where the Spanish first landed in Mexico in the sixteenth century, the area now has the fewest tourists. The city of Veracruz is a seaport, famous for its hot, humid weather, its colonial architecture—and its excellent seafood!

¿Sabes que...?

★ The Mexican name for the river that marks the US-Mexican border is **el río Bravo del Norte**.

El centro

Estados: Estado de México, Hidalgo, Querétaro. Distrito Federal: la ciudad de México (México DF).

Some people say Mexico City is the biggest city in the world! The area around this capital city has a high concentration of industry and is the most heavily populated part of the country.

Nearby there is fine scenery with mountains and forests, villages famous for their handicrafts (pottery, rugs, shawls), and many archeological sites, including spectacular Teotihuacán. In the mountains, several national parks have been created.

Querétaro is Mexico's most historic city. It was part of the Aztec empire, later becoming an important colonial town. Secret plans for Mexican independence were made there, and the Treaty of Guadalupe Hidalgo, ceding California and New Mexico to the United States in 1848, was ratified there. In June, 1867, the Emperor Maximilian was executed in the city. The present constitution was written there in 1917.

This region is a high plateau crossed by mountains. Mexico City is 7,200 feet (2,195 meters) above sea level. There are a number of volcanoes, including Popocatépetl (17,887 feet/5,452 meters).

México, D.F.

El volcán Ixtaccihuatl

Sudeste

Estados: Tabasco, Chiapas, Campeche, Yucatán, Quintana Roo

The low-lying Yucatán peninsula is flat and tropical. To tourists, it is best known for the spectacular snow-white beaches of Cozumel and Isla Mujeres, and for the new resort of Cancún.

Mérida, state capital of the Yucatán, is a city of Spanish colonial and 19th-century French-style buildings, built by rich landowners and merchants. Until well into this century, the most convenient way to reach Mexico City from Mérida was to take a ship to Veracruz, and from there to go by road to the capital. The city's wealth and former isolation gave it, and the region, a sense of independence from the rest of Mexico.

This is the land of the Mayas, who built the ancient sites of Uxmal, Chichén Itzá, and Tulum. Many of the local Indians still speak the Mayan language.

Mérida, la ciudad blanca

La ciudad de Acapulco, Guerrero

El sitio arqueológico de Mitla, Oaxaca

Ready to go

¿Qué tiempo hace?

The climate in Mexico changes with altitude. The hottest parts, **la tierra caliente**, are the coasts, especially along the Gulf Coast, and plateau areas below 3,000 feet (914 meters). There is a temperate area, **la tierra templada**, between 3,000 and 8,500 feet (914m–2,591m). The coldest part, **la tierra fría**, is land over 8,500 feet (2,591m).

There are two seasons—wet (May to October) and dry (November to April). May is usually the hottest month.

In Mexico City, 7,200 feet above sea level, the days are generally warm and the evenings cool, with afternoon showers in the wet season. On the coast, the days are sunny and the evenings warm, although it can be very hot and humid during the day in the wet season.

● In Spanish, tell which area Mexico City is in.

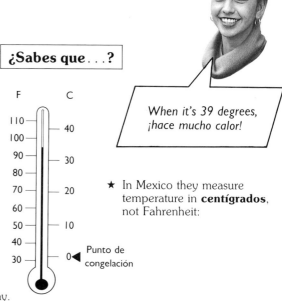

¿Sabes que...?

When it's 39 degrees, ¡hace mucho calor!

★ In Mexico they measure temperature in **centígrados**, not Fahrenheit:

Punto de congelación

¿Cómo se dice?

● With a partner, say in Spanish what the weather is like today.

Hace calor.	Hace sol.	Está lloviendo.	Está nublado.	Hace frío.	

¿Qué tiempo hace?

Está lloviendo.

Mexicans appreciate smart clothes. In the cities, casual clothes (but not shorts and beach wear) are good for day time. Evenings tend to be more formal. In resorts, beach wear is good for hotels and beaches, and stylish casual clothes for the evenings.

This is a weather forecast for Mexico.
● How many weather zones is the country divided into?
● Which town is expected to have the highest temperature? Which zone is it in?
● Which zone will have the lowest temperature?
● Which towns will have clouds and rain, but the temperature will stay the same?
● Which season do you think the forecast is for?

EL CLIMA, HOY

ZONA NOROESTE
CALUROSO, Nublado con lluvias por la tarde y vientos moderados del sureste. La Temperatura más alta se registrará en Mexicali con 39 grados Centígrados.

ZONA NORTE
SIN cambios en la temperatura, nublado con algunas lluvias en Chihuahua y Durango. Vientos moderados del suroeste.

ZONA CENTRO
MEDIO nublado en la mañana y por la tarde y noche se registrarán lluvias. En el Valle de México, la temperatura máxima será de 21 a 23° C. y la mínima de 11 a 13.

ZONA ORIENTE
CALUROSO, medio nublado, lluvias escasas y vientos moderados del este.

What to take

Tony and his sister Maria are both going to Mexico in April. As you can see, they have different attitudes toward packing.

anteojos de sol
corbata
traje de baño
toalla
loción bronceadora
shorts
cepillo de dientes
sandalias

chamarra
abrigo
cámara
pantalón
maleta
medias
zapatos
camisa
paraguas
diccionario
falda

Tony es optimista.   **María es pesimista.**

- Make a list in Spanish of the things you think Tony should have packed.
- What does Maria need? Does she have anything that's unnecessary?
- What toiletries would you add to your list—in Spanish?

Tips for packing

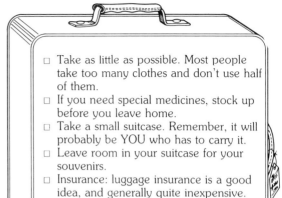

- ☐ Take as little as possible. Most people take too many clothes and don't use half of them.
- ☐ If you need special medicines, stock up before you leave home.
- ☐ Take a small suitcase. Remember, it will probably be YOU who has to carry it.
- ☐ Leave room in your suitcase for your souvenirs.
- ☐ Insurance: luggage insurance is a good idea, and generally quite inexpensive. Also, check whether your regular medical insurance covers you in Mexico.

Do some of these look familiar? The bottle on the left is Tehuacán, pure mineral water. Try some of the fruit drinks, too!

El turista

A sudden change in food and water and a lot of traveling can occasionally cause an upset stomach or headache. Mexicans often call these stomach upsets **el turista**, but they are not exclusive to Mexico. With some common sense, you shouldn't get sick:

- ☐ Eat in clean restaurants, preferably those that deal regularly with tourists.
- ☐ Don't buy food from stalls or street vendors...no matter how good it smells!
- ☐ Where possible, avoid tap water, ice and ice cream. Hotels have bottles of purified water, and commercially-bottled water is easy to find in the shops.
- ☐ Medical opinion differs about the benefit of patent medicines. If you are worried, ask your own doctor about medication before you leave home.

Most visitors to Mexico—who are sensible—don't get sick. If you are unlucky, and a couple of hours' rest has not set things right, ask your hotel to call a doctor. He should be able to give you a prescription.

If you need something from **una farmacia** (drugstore), many brand names are often the same as at home. The sales assistant in **la farmacia** can help you.

Passport, please?

Canadian and US visitors entering Mexico don't even have to show passports. They can use a certificate of nationality, birth certificate or voter's registration for identification. Having a passport, however, does generally make things much easier. Visitors from other countries must have passports.

Every tourist needs a tourist permit, **una tarjeta de turista**, which allows visits of up to 180 days. US and Canadian visitors arriving by air can get these from the airline or from their travel agents. Visitors from other countries need tourist permits approved by a Mexican consulate.

La cocina mexicana

Traditional Mexican food

Tenemos platos ricos—y picantes—en México. Nos gusta comer en buena compañía—en familia o con amigos.

*I love **tacos** and **enchiladas**.*

Hay otras cosas buenas para comer. ¡A mí me gusta el mole poblano!

Many traditional dishes like **tacos** and **enchiladas** are made with **tortillas**. This thin cornmeal bread has been eaten in Mexico since the earliest days of the Indian civilizations. Tortillas are used in many dishes:
- eaten plain instead of bread.
- with fillings (cheese, meat, vegetables, beans) to make **tacos**, **enchiladas**, **sopes** and **chilaquiles**.
- served with **huevos rancheros** (fried eggs and a tomato chili sauce on top).
- as **totopos** (fried and cut into small triangles) for eating **frijoles refritos** (refried beans) or **guacamole** (a mixture of avocado, tomatoes, chilies, onion, salt and coriander).

    Tacos, **enchiladas** and **chilaquiles** may be served with salad, **frijoles refritos** and **guacamole**. There's usually a bowl of **salsa mexicana** (chopped tomato, onion, chilies and fresh coriander) on the table. You can use it to liven up what you're eating. There will often be a plate of cut limes as well to add flavor to different dishes. Sometimes you'll find **chiles en vinagre** which are pickled pieces of chilies, carrots, onions and cauliflower.

The word **mole** means ground or mashed food. For example, **guacamole** is a kind of dip whose main ingredient is **aguacate** (avocado). **Mole poblano** is a sauce made of chocolate, nuts, chilies and other spices, and served with turkey (**pavo**), chicken, pork or **enchiladas**. It is for special occasions, like family reunions or weddings.

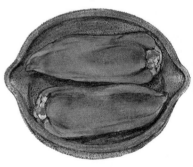

*Another typical dish is **chiles rellenos**. These are peppers fried and stuffed with ground beef, cheese, beans, or tuna.*

Tortillas are often bought from a shop because grinding up corn kernels to make the dough is a very time-consuming job. **Left***: tortilla dough.* **Right***: Freshly made tortillas are kept moist and warm in a cloth.*

● What can you see on this plate?

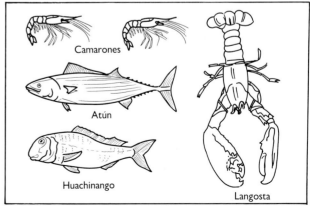

Camarones

Atún

Huachinango

Langosta

Fish and seafood are excellent. These are some of the varieties that you can find.

¡Qué buena fruta!

The fruit in Mexico is excellent. Try **una ensalada de frutas**, a fruit salad made with papaya or mangoes. You might prefer a **licuado**, a refreshing fresh fruit shake blended with water or milk.

- Look at the list of **licuados** above.
  1 Are the **licuados** made with water or with milk?
  2 There are two kinds of **licuados** made from watermelon and from melon. What is the Spanish word for watermelon?
  3 One of the **licuados** is not made from a fruit. Which one is it?

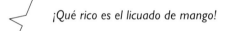

¡Qué rico es el licuado de mango!

¡Mira!

☞ See how many different tropical fruits you can find in the shops and supermarket where you live. Do any of them come from Mexico?

☞ There are big food markets in Mexico, but many people buy from **supermercados** (supermarkets) and grocery stores. Try to visit a Mexican supermarket. How many brands can you recognize?

☞ Collect some candy wrappers and labels for your souvenir album.

These candy bars are sold in Mexico. **Rompope** is a liqueur made from eggs and flavored with vanilla.
- What are the other flavors?

¿Sabes que. . .?

★ In stores, food and drink are sold in **gramos**, **kilos** and **litros**. Do you know what the equivalents are in ounces, pounds and pints?

On the breakfast menu

DESAYUNO
FRUTAS
Orden de Frutas Frescas
Media Toronja
Compota de Ciruelas
CEREALES:
Avena con Leche
Crema de Trigo
Corn Flakes o Rice Krispies
con Plátano
HUEVOS Y ESPECIALIDADES:
Dos Huevos al Gusto
Con: Jamón, Tocino o Salchicha
Tortilla a la Española
Huevos Rancheros o Mexicana
Omelette de Champiñones o Jamón
Omelette Natural
Chilaquiles con Pollo Gratinados
Orden de Jamón, Tocino o Salchicha
HOT CAKES Y PANES:
Pan Tostado Francés
Hot Cakes
Con: Tocino, Jamón o Salchicha
Canasta de Pan Dulce (3)
Café, Té o Leche

Look at this breakfast menu.
- What English words have slipped into Spanish?
- Choose a light breakfast.
- Order a special Mexican breakfast.
- Can you find some things that you have for breakfast?

¿Qué desea beber?

Match the names to the drinks:

Vino	**Café**
Agua	**Refresco**
Jugo de fruta	**Cerveza**
Té	

¡Pruebe! **Chocolate**: Made with water or milk, it's delicious!
Atole: Yet another way in which cornmeal is used, this time for a hot drink flavoured with cinnamon and vanilla.

Families, festivals and student life

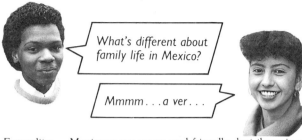

What's different about family life in Mexico?

Mmmm...a ver...

Una familia mexicana

Formality: Mexicans are warm and friendly, but there is a tradition of formal good manners.

Meals: Eating together as a family is important. People tend to eat fewer fast food meals and snacks than in America.

Servants: Many Mexican homes have domestic help.

Children: Children are very important members of the family. At family parties, they are introduced properly, mingle with guests and stay up late. They are expected to behave well.

Teenagers: The idea that there is something different about young people between the ages of 13 and 19 doesn't exist. Young people are treated either as children or young adults.

Dating: Individual dating is discouraged by parents.

Boys and girls tend to go out with groups of friends. Often a girl is only allowed out with a boy, if her brother goes along.

Large families: Often several generations share the family home. There is no lack of company—or advice! There's lots of help and support and finding baby-sitters is never a problem.

Estar en fiestas

There are parties and celebrations for special occasions in Mexican families.

At the age of three, children are dressed up and attend a special church service in their honor, **la Presentación de tres años**.

Between seven and 12 years of age, children make their first communion. It's an occasion to celebrate with family and friends.

Weddings are not just the joining of two people, but the alliance of two families, so they are celebrated with great formality. Weddings in well-known families are often written up in great detail in the newspapers.

Piñatas are always popular with children, especially at birthday parties. Originally, they were decorated earthenware jars filled with candy, fruit and peanuts. Now they are made of cardboard often in the shapes of animals. The **piñata** is hung from a rope and children take turns at hitting it with a stick to bring down a shower of sweets on the children below.

When a girl reaches 15, there is a special party or ball for her. She is the center of attention—for a day.

- What services are offered in these ads?
- Can they do weddings and fifteenth birthday parties?
- What other family events are mentioned?

En la clase

There are four levels:
- **primaria**: six to 12 years.
- **secundaria**: 12 to 16 years.
- **preparatoria**: 16 to 19 years.
- **universitaria**: 19 plus.

There are state schools everywhere, even in remote parts of the country. In the big cities, there are many private schools. The school year runs from September to June.

This is a sign outside a private ▶ school.
- Is the school coed?
- Would children below the age of 12 study here?
- As well as **secundaria** and **preparatoria**, what other courses does this school offer?

HORA	LUNES	MARTES	MIERCOLES	JUEVES	VIERNES 1o. "B"
7:00–8:00	FISICA	LECTURA	FISICA (LAB) "B"		
8:00–9:00	DEPORTES	LECTURA	FISICA (LAB) "B"	REDACCION	FISICA
9:00–10:00	REDACCION	MATEMATICAS	FISICA	MATEMATICAS	MATEMATICAS
10:00–11:00	REDACCION	TALLER	INGLES	TALLER	MATEMATICAS
11:00–12:00	INGLES	TALLER	DEPORTES	TALLER	INGLES
12:00–13:00	HISTORIA		HISTORIA	DEPORTES	
13:00–14:00	HISTORIA				

◄ Look at this schedule for a student in the third year of **secundaria**. Students often take a quick break for a snack at 10.00 or 10.30 am.
- Can you recognize all the courses?
- What subjects are offered that are not offered in your school?
- How do the hours compare with yours?

¡Mira!

☞ Try to visit a Mexican school. What is different from your high school?

Entrevista

These are excerpts from interviews with two Mexican teenagers who are talking about their likes and dislikes.

❝ Me llamo Vicente y tengo 17 años. Estoy en el primer año de preparatoria.

¿Adónde voy yo para divertirme? Me gusta mucho salir con mis amigos para comer en algún restaurante, o ir al cine.

Juego en un equipo de futbol y tomo lecciones en un club de karate.

El año pasado fui a visitar a mi primo que trabaja en los Estados Unidos. Durante aquellas tres semanas practiqué mi inglés, y quisiera volver allí para aprender más. ❞

❝ Yo soy Concha. Tengo 15 años. Estoy en la secundaria. ¿Qué me gusta hacer? Me gusta pasar tiempo con mis amigas y me gusta ir a la costa.

Espero ir a la universidad y tener una carrera. Pero tal vez me case también y tenga hijos. ¿Qué me enoja? ¡Que mis padres siempre dan más libertad a mi hermano! ❞

- Does Vicente like sports?
- What annoys Concha?
- Where does Vicente's cousin live?
- Does Concha like vacations in the countryside?
- Write something in Spanish about yourself.

Settling in

Recién llegado

Airports may be a long way from the centre of the city. To get to your hotel you can take a taxi or a **colectivo**. It's called **un colectivo** because, for a small set fare, you share a car or a VW van with other people going to the same destination.

HOTEL AMBASSADOR

HUMBOLDT Núm. 38
06050-MEXICO, D. F.

TEL. 518-01-10
TELEX 017-76-276-AMBAM

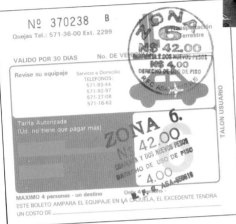

Nº 370238 B
Quejas Tel.: 571-36-00 Ext. 2299

VALIDO POR 30 DIAS   No. DE VE...

Revise su equipaje   Servicio a Domicilio
TELEFONOS:
571-93-44
571-92-97
571-27-08
571-16-62

ZONA 6.
M$ 42.00

Tarifa Autorizada
(Ud. no tiene que pagar más)

MAXIMO 4 personas - un destino   Only 4 persons
ESTE BOLETO AMPARA EL EQUIPAJE EN LA CAJUELA, EL EXCEDENTE TENDRA
UN COSTO DE ...

At Mexico City Airport you pay for the taxi in advance by buying a special ticket. Fares are set according to zone, so give your destination.
● Which zone is this ticket for?
● What should you do with your baggage?
● Should you have to pay more for the taxi ride?

This is a card for a hotel in Mexico.
● What's different about the way the street name and number are written?
● What city is the hotel in?

¿Qué clase de hotel es?

These people have very different ideas about what they want from a hotel. Look at these hotel ads and select a hotel for each of them.

Necesitamos un hotel grande en la costa para nuestra convención anual.

¡Me encanta ir a la playa!

Me apasionan las ciudades históricas.

Buscamos algo tranquilo—y económico—para toda la familia.

HOTEL EL MIRADOR
"LA MEJOR VISTA AL PACIFICO"
85 HABITACIONES   ESTACIONAMIENTO
RESTAURANT   JARDINES
RESERVACIONES:
91 (958)
2-03-59   2-03-98
2-01-29   2-02-31
PONIENTE No. 113 CARR. COSTERA DEL PACIFICO
A UNOS CUANTOS PASOS DE LA PLAYA
PUERTO ESCONDIDO, OAX.

HOTELES CANADA
SU HOGAR EN GUADALAJARA
ECONOMICOS, FAMILIARES Y
CONFORTABLES
ESTACIONAMIENTO PROPIO,
RESTAURANT - BAÑOS - VAPOR
SAUNA
DR R. MICHEL 215   19-20-92
ESTADIO 77   19-40-14
GUADALAJARA, JAL

INCREIBLEMENTE
ECONOMICOS
Hoteles
Nueva Galicia.
EN EL CENTRO DE LA CIUDAD
Habitaciones totalmente alfombradas, con T V, Teléfono, F.M.
aire acondicionado, servi-bar, restaurant-bar y estacionamiento

LA TRADICION EN PUEBLA
NATURALMENTE
Hotel Lastra
UBICADO EN LA ZONA HISTORICA DE LA CIUDAD
RESTAURANT - BAR - ALBERCA
CONFORTABLES HABITACIONES
CON F.M. Y T V. A COLOR
SALONES PARA BANQUETES Y CONVENCIONES
HERMOSOS JARDINES
CALZ. DE LOS FUERTES 2633   (LADA 91-22)
PUEBLA, PUE.   35-97-55

UN HOTEL PARA EJECUTIVOS
188 HABITACIONES DE LUJO
4 MASTERS SUITES
Y 8 JUNIOR SUITES
TERRANOVA
hotel club
RESTAURANT - BAR - PISCINA - CLUB DE PLAYA
"LA PALAPA" - HELIPUERTO - DISCOTHEQUE - TENIS
SALA DE CONVENCIONES HASTA PARA 400 PERSONAS
ESTACIONAMIENTO PROPIO
CANALES DE T.V. COLOR POR SATELITE

¿Cómo se dice?

Look at the symbols from this hotel's brochure and answer the clients' queries.

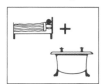   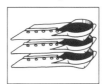

SERVICIO DE CUARTOS

CAMBIO

LARGA DISTANCIA

AIRE ACONDICIONADO

- Look at the symbols again. With a partner, practice asking:
  - if you can change money.
  - if there is a room with bath.
  - if there is room service.

- When would you hang this on your door?

FAVOR DE NO MOLESTAR

PLAZA VALLARTA
TENNIS & BEACH RESORT

¡Mira!

☞ Watch a few minutes of Mexican TV in your hotel room. What kind of programs can you see?
☞ The faucets in your room will be marked **C** and **F**. What do these letters stand for?
☞ In your hotel look for information about the hotel, the city or the country. What is available?
☞ Collect match book covers, place mats, and coasters as souvenirs.

¿Sabes que...?

★ At ground level the elevator is marked PB for **planta baja**. The first floor in Mexico is the one above ground level.

★ Making long distance calls abroad from a hotel can be expensive.

Sad reality

Poverty and unemployment are sad realities for many Mexicans, but they're not unique to Mexico. You will be asked for money. Do as Mexicans do; if you want to help, keep coins handy in your pocket. But don't feel that you've got to take the weight of the whole world's problems on your shoulders.

A visit to Mexico City

Vamos a dar una vuelta por México, la capital más grande del mundo.

Remember Mexico City is more than 7,000 feet (2,000 m) above sea level, and you need time to get used to the altitude. Don't rush around. Take it easy for the first few days until you feel at home.

This statue is a monument to independence on **el Paseo de la Reforma**, an important avenue running east-west through the city. It intersects with **Avenida Insurgentes**, another avenue running north-south.

¿Conoces el mapa de la ciudad?

Este mapa muestra algunos sitios interesantes en el centro de la ciudad.

¿Dónde está la catedral?

Seis cuadras todo derecho y estará usted en el Zócalo. La catedral está enfrente.

Estoy buscando la Casa de los Azulejos.

1 Alameda Central
2 Museo de Artes Populares
3 Palacio de Bellas Artes
4 Correo Mayor
5 Torre Latinoamericana
6 Casa de los Azulejos
7 Palacio de Iturbide
8 Edificio Nacional Monte de Piedad
9 Catedral Metropolitana
10 Templo Mayor
11 Portal de Mercaderes
12 Plaza de la Constitución (Zócalo)
13 Palacio Nacional

Una cuadra más y dos cuadras a la izquierda. Se encuentra a la derecha en la esquina de Madero y Condesa.

Give directions from where you are to someone who wants to go to:
– the Alameda Park.
– the central post office.

¿Sabes que . . . ?

★ Mexico City is divided into 16 areas called **delegaciones**. The historic center around the Zócalo is in **la delegación Cuauhtémoc**.

▲ This brochure has information about the city center.

MUSEO DE LA FALSIFICACION

Colecciones de billetes falsos, máquinas y equipo para su impresión, cliches, moldes para monedas, instrumentos para dibujar y otras herramientas para la falsificación se presentan en este lugar.

Ubicación: Marconi 2 - 1er. piso esq. Tacuba.
Días de visita: Lunes a Viernes
Horario: 9:00 a 17:00 Hrs.
Duración del recorrido: 30 minutos
Entrada: Libre

Here is some information about an unusual museum.
● What can you see there?
● How long does it take to go around?
● How much does it cost to go in?
● Use the location details given to find out where the museum is on the map above.

¡Vámonos!

Recuerdo del Mirador más alto
de Latinoamérica
(2422 metros sobre el nivel del mar)
México, D.F.

Once the tallest building in the city, **la Torre Latinoamericana** is still a good vantage point from which to look out over Mexico City. It is a few blocks from **el Zócalo**, a very large square at the center of the city. **La Torre** has a specially designed foundation to prevent any sinking due to the soft subsoil and to resist earth tremors. In the 1985 earthquake, it resisted tremors up to force 8 on the Richter scale.

El Palacio de Bellas Artes is the city's principal theater and one of its most important concert halls. It is also an art museum with murals by Diego Rivera, David Alfaro Siqueiros and José Clemente Orozco. It is also the home of **el Ballet folklórico de México**.

In the southwest of the city is **la Universidad Autónoma de México (UNAM)**. The 41-million-square-foot (3.8 million-square-meter) complex features the work of many modern Mexican artists, including Rivera and Siqueiros. The central library (right) is decorated with mosaics designed by Juan O'Gorman.

On Sundays, join Mexicans as they stroll, jog, attend open-air classes and picnic in **el Bosque de Chapultepec**, the world's largest city park. It is also the oldest in the Americas and has eight museums, three lakes, botanical gardens, a zoo, an amusement park and **los Pinos**, the President's official residence. On a hill in the park is **el Castillo de Chapultepec** which houses **el Museo Nacional de Historia** with exhibits and murals about Mexico's past.

El Museo Nacional de Antropología e Historia (MNAH) contains artifacts from pre-Columbian cultures, as well as present-day folk exhibits. The museum's central patio has a concrete roof held up by a single bronze sculptured pillar. Mexicans call this **el paraguas** (umbrella).

Mexico City is closely linked to its pre-Columbian past—the historic center around **el Zócalo** was the former ceremonial main plaza of the Aztec city of Tenochtitlán. The ruins of **el Templo Mayor**, an ancient Aztec temple, were discovered as recently as 1978 when new electrical cables were being laid.

Getting around town

Caminar es lindo para conocer una ciudad. Se ve como vive la gente. A veces es más facil tomar un camión o tal vez un taxi.

¿En autobús o en taxi?

In Mexico the word **camión** is used for a bus or a truck, but people will understand if you say **bus**. Bus fares are charged according to the distance you travel. When you get on the bus, give your destination and the driver will tell you how much to pay.

For Mexico City public buses the bus route and destination are usually indicated on the bus shelter.
● Where does route 76 go to?
● One route runs along Reforma. Along which street does the other run?

There are three types of taxi in Mexico City. **Turismo** *taxis operate from outside first-class hotels. Taxis from bus terminals, the airport and railroad stations have no meters. Passengers pay in advance at a ticket booth. The price of a journey is calculated by zone. Yellow or green taxis have meters. Green taxis usually use lead-free gasoline.*

¿Sabes que...?

★ Only Mexico and Brazil still manufacture VW Bugs. They are popular for use as taxis and several thousand are produced every year. Mexicans call them **vochos**.

Colectivos or **peseros** are a cross between a bus and a taxi. Cars or VW vans, they run on fixed routes along the main avenues and principal routes in and out of towns. Routes are shown on a card in the windscreen and there are set fares. In Mexico City **colectivos** are green.
● What warning is on the back of this **colectivo**?

As in many modern cities, traffic is a problem in Mexico City, not only for the inconvenience it causes, but also because of pollution. The federal district government tries to encourage drivers to leave their cars at home one day a week.
● What is the government campaign called?
● What day of the week would you leave your car at home with this sticker?

En el metro

El metro is a quick way of getting around town. Since Line 1 went into service in September 1969, nine more lines have been added. When excavations were being made for the subway, many Aztec remains were discovered. Some are on display in subway stations like **Pino Suárez**.

Every day 4.5 million people use the subway and, in terms of the number of people it transports, it is third in the world after Moscow and Tokyo. In the rush hours trains are very crowded. Avoid the worst of it by traveling between 10 am and 4 pm.

You can travel as far as you like with one ticket, provided you do not pass through an exit barrier.

☞ Each station has a symbol. Chapultepec has a grasshopper, because the station name is the Aztec word for 'grasshopper'.

This map shows the subway network. For a journey from **Hospital General** on **Línea 3** to **Politécnico** on **Línea 5**, take **Línea 3, dirección Indios Verdes**. Change at **La Raza** and look for the orange **correspondencia** or yellow **dirección Politécnico** signs.

Each subway line uses a different color for its signs. **Línea 5** is yellow. Where there is a **correspondencia** between lines, the indicator sign for the line shows the colors of both lines. In most stations there are **módulos de información** where subway maps and information can be obtained.

- Plan a route from:
  — Tlatelolco to the airport.
  — Balderas to Consulado (two possible ways)

- Metro stations are often named for famous people.
  a Who are the Aztec emperors on **Línea 1**?
  b Who is the Mexican president on **Línea 9**?
  c Which leader from the independence struggle is on **Líneas 2/3**?

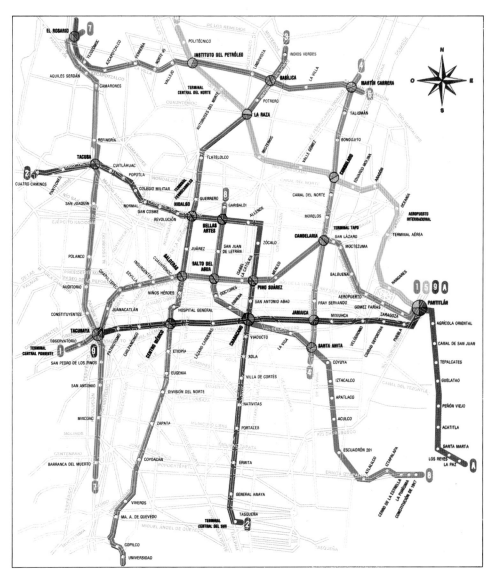

Some cities in Mexico

La patria chica

Mexicans are very proud of the particular city or region where they live. The place they originate from is often known as **la tierra** (literally 'the land') or **la patria chica** (small homeland), as opposed to **la patria grande** which is the Republic of Mexico.

Often people from a particular region are given a special nickname. An inhabitant of the Federal District is **un chilango**, while someone from Guadalajara could be **un tapatío** or **un jalisciense** (from the state of Jalisco). If you come from Jalapa, you are **un jalapeño**! Someone who lives in Veracruz is **un jarocho**.

- Why is the golf and tennis club on the right called **El Tapatío**?

Guadalajara

Known as **la Perla de Occidente**, Guadalajara is Mexico's second largest city, with about four million inhabitants. Founded in 1542, the city was named for the Spanish city of Guadalajara, the home town of Nuño Beltrádé Guzmán, the first conquistador to explore the surrounding area.

As well as being the center of a rich agricultural area, Guadalajara has a large industrial zone. Mariachi music is said to have originated in Jalisco, the state surrounding Guadalajara.

This is what a young **tapatía** says about her city.

« Me llamo María Angélica. Soy de Guadalajara y es mi ciudad favorita. Me gusta porque hay de todo. La parte vieja alrededor de la Plaza de Armas es bonita, pero Guadalajara también es una ciudad moderna y dinámica.

Cerca de la ciudad hay muchos lugares interesantes, sobre todo el lago de Chapala.

Mire usted las fotos y verá algunos lugares de interés para los que visitan la ciudad. »

El Teatro Degollado, construido en 1856, en la tradición de los grandes teatros europeos

Cuernavaca

Famous for its year-round pleasant climate and its flowers, Cuernavaca is sometimes called **la ciudad de la primavera eterna**. It owes its pleasant climate to the fact that it lies 2,000 feet (734 meters) lower than Mexico City.

Since Aztec times it has offered a retreat from the rigors of the capital. In 1530, Cortés retired to a palace he had built in the city. Many people, including those who had made their fortunes in the silver mines of Taxco, built houses there. One such house, belonging to José de la Borda, was a favorite haven of Emperor Maximilian and Empress Carlotta. Today, there is a large community of Americans who have retirement homes in the city.

« ¿Quiere Vd conocer Cuernavaca? Yo soy Antonio. Tengo un taxi. No vivo en la ciudad, pero vivo cerca. Salí para ver otras partes del país, pero siempre he vuelto aquí. Me gusta el ambiente y la gente interesante que se encuentra aquí. ¡Mire las fotos! ¿Quiere usted ver la catedral o desea un hotel bueno? ¡Yo le llevo! »

Acapulco

Acapulco grew up around its great natural harbor. In colonial times it was the main port of the West Coast. Many expeditions exploring other parts of **Nueva España** set sail from here. After 1565, **naos** (galleons) from Manila landed Chinese and Japanese goods here. These were then carried overland by mule to Veracruz for shipment to Spain. Pirates, especially from England, preyed on shipping along the Pacific coast and in 1616 the fort of San Diego was built on the hill overlooking the bay.

After independence, trade declined until the 1920s when a road was built linking Acapulco to inland cities. After World War II, Acapulco (the nearest West Coast city to the capital) boomed as a resort for Mexican and foreign tourists.

La bahía de Acapulco, sitio de las pruebas de vela de los Juegos Olímpicos de 1968

" Ramón Sánchez, a sus órdenes. Bienvenidos a Acapulco, mi ciudad. Mi familia llegó aquí hace cincuenta años. ¡Se han efectuado muchos cambios desde entonces! Para muchas personas Acapulco es solamente un lugar adonde ir de vacaciones; pero yo vivo y trabajo aquí. La foto les muestra un aspecto de la ciudad. **"**

¡Mira!

☞ There are many regional newspapers. Find a copy of the local paper for the area you are staying in. What's it called?

El palacio de Cortés

In the evenings, **la plaza de armas**, the main square, is the place where the whole family comes to listen to bands playing in the bandstand or to stroll around.

Signs and ads

En el parque

Which signs should these people have looked at while they were out in the park?

> If you don't understand the words on signs and ads, use clues like the pictures or the place where a sign is to help you.

 A

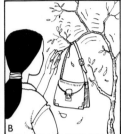 B

 C

 D

①
PARA EL BIENESTAR DE TODOS EN PARQUES Y JARDINES SOLO CON CADENA

② Las áreas verdes, árboles y plantas son tuyos, cuidalos.
AYUNTAMIENTO GUADALAJARA 1986-1988

④
NO PASE AREA EN REFORESTACION POR FAVOR CUIDALA TU AMIGO EL BOSQUE

③
AVISO NO BEBA EL AGUA DE RIEGO

Carteleras

- What are these billboards advertising?

¡No estacionarse!

Finding a parking space is a problem in all big cities. The **E** on the no parking sign means **estacionarse**.

Look at this sign and explain why parking is not allowed...

ENTRADA — E — NO ESTACIONARSE

SE USARA GRUA

- What will happen if a car is illegally parked?

- This notice is outside a private house. What are the residents threatening to do if a car is illegally parked?

E — * SE * PONCHAN LLANTAS NO GRATIS

¡Mira!

☞ If you see an unusual billboard or poster, take a photo of it. What is it advertising?

Llamar la atención

Sometimes businesses use eye-catching ideas to attract the attention of customers.
- What kind of businesses are these?
- Are the ideas for attracting clients good ones?

Se vende

Look at these small ads from a newspaper.
- What section would you expect to find them in?
- In what part of northern Mexico can you buy a ranch?
- You have a small house. What could you exchange it for in Mexico City?
- You're looking for a 4-bedroom house. There are two being offered here, but in which parts of Mexico?
- You're looking for a piece of land with a good water supply. Where is someone offering one at a 'give-away' price?

GUADALAJARA, JAL.

CASA
En Colonia guadalupana, de 2 Plantas, 4 Recámaras, Sala Comedor, Teléfono, Cochera.
30-07-02

PUEBLA, PUE.
VENDO TERRENO
Precio Regalado: 25 Hectáreas en **El Seco**, Mucha Agua. Informan 40-10-12, 43-07-55

GUADALAJARA, JAL.
URGENTE VENDO
Departamento Tres Recámaras, Planta Baja, Teléfono, Estatuto Jurídico Zapopan, Recibo Carro, **32-47-75, 31-45-40**

CULIACAN, SIN.
VENDO
Casa Cuatro Recámaras Cochera Para Tres Carros.
Informes 5-18-34 y 3-03-92

PARRAL, COAH.
SE VENDE
Rancho 6,095 Hectáreas, Ubicado en Durango, Varios Potreros, Agua, Instalaciones, Buen Agostadero.
Informes Teléfono 2-29-50

VENDO
Departamento en D.F. Cerca de Zona Rosa, Acepto, Cambio por Casa Chica Informes
Teléfono 2-25-69

SE VENDE
Hermosa Huerta Manzanera, 9,000 Arboles en Producción Guerrero Chih. Equipada Totalmente Informes
Teléfonos 6-03-05; 6-04-15 Guerrero, Chih.

Indicadores

Find the Spanish words from this list to go with each of these signs.

Información turística   **Agua para lavarse las manos**   **¡Cuidado! ¡Escuela!**   **¡No pase!**

① ② ③ ④

37

¡Buen provecho!

En México hay restaurantes de todo tipo.

- Where can you eat spaghetti bolognese?
- Which restaurant serves Argentinian food?
- What does Zapata offer as well as Mexican and international food?

La cuenta

A 10 percent federal sales tax has to be paid on food in hotels and restaurants. **IVA (Impuesto sobre valor agregado)** is often included in the prices on the menu, but some restaurants list the tax separately on the check. It is not a service charge. Another 15 percent as **una propina** (a tip) would be appreciated.

CAFE de TACUBA
CENTRO. S. A.

| TACUBA 28 | | MEXICO 1, D. F. |
| CED. I. M. 1290665 | | REG. FED. CAUS. CTC-840424 |

	Café con leche	
Sírvia	Bizcochos	Pasas
	Cerveza	

Sub. Total
I.V.A. 10%
N° 36654 **TOTAL**

COPIA PARA EL CONSUMIDOR

¿Cómo se dice?

Sometimes when a restaurant is busy, the waiter may not have time to come and speak to you right away. To show that s/he has seen you, s/he may make this sign. It means **un momento** (just a moment). You might even use it yourself if you can't think of how to say something in Spanish and want a little time to think.

¿Sabes que...?

★ **Tortas** are not pastries, they are sandwiches served in a flat bun.

Una comida corrida is a set meal with **un plato del día** (a daily special) that is served usually between 1 and 4 pm. If you want a wider selection, you can choose your meal from **la carta**.

¿Qué quiere comer?

A la carta

SOPAS

Sopa Especial de Pollo Denny's

Sopa de Tortilla

Sopa del Día

Sopa de Verduras Frescas

ENSALADAS

Nuestra Ensalada Especial del Chef
Lechuga, gajos de jitomate, tiras de jamón, pollo y queso, rebanadas de huevo cocido.

Ensalada de Camarones
Lechuga, gajos de jitomate, camarones frescos, huevo cocido.

Ensalada de Pollo
Lechuga, gajos de jitomate, dos cucharones de pollo aderezado y huevo cocido.

Ensalada de Atún
Lechuga, gajos de jitomate, atún aderezado y huevo cocido.

Ensalada de Lechuga, Jitomate y Pepino

BEBIDAS
Nuestro Famoso Café Denny's
Té Caliente o Helado   Leche
Chocolate Caliente   Naranjada
Chocolate Frío   Limonada
Refrescos

ESPECIALIDADES MEXICANAS

Tacos de Pollo (4)
Servidos con guacamole, crema y frijoles refritos.

Tacos de Bistec (3)
Acompañados de cebollitas de cambray asadas, servido con frijoles charros.

Costilla de Res a la Parrilla
Servida con chilaquiles y frijoles charros.

Plato Mexicano
Puntas de cerdo en salsa ranchera o chipotle, servidas con arroz, enchilada, guacamole y frijoles refritos.

Pepitos (2)
Tierno filete de res en bolillos, acompañado de guacamole, frijoles refritos, rajas con crema y papas a la francesa.

Chilaquiles Verdes o Rojos
Gratinados con queso y servidos con crema, cebolla y frijoles refritos.
Con pollo.
Con pollo y huevo.

ENCHILADAS

Enchiladas Suizas
Elaboradas con pollo y salsa suiza, preparadas con nuestra receta especial.

Enchiladas Verdes o Rojas
Preparadas con pollo, queso al gratín y una generosa porción de salsas deliciosamente condimentadas.

Enchiladas de Mole
Elaboradas con pollo, ajonjolí, cebolla y delicioso mole poblano.

CARROUSEL DE HAMBURGUESAS

Dennyburger
Servida con jitomate y lechuga.
Con queso

Combinación Denny's
Riquísima hamburguesa acompañada de papas a la francesa. A su elección, sopa del día o ensalada con aderezo Dennys.

Combinación Denny's Gigante
Riquísima hamburguesa de 200 gramos, acompañada de papas a la francesa. A su elección, sopa del día o ensalada con aderezo Denny's.

Hamburguesa Mexicana
Servida con frijoles refritos, salsa chipotle, cebollas fritas, hoja de lechuga y rebanada de jitomate.

Plato Dieta
Hamburguesa en pan de centeno, acompañada de queso cotage, rebanada de jitomate y huevo cocido.

CARNES, AVES Y PESCADO

Parrillada Mixta
Preparado con filete de res, pollo, cerdo y chorizo, servida con guacamole, frijoles charros y tortillas.

Pechuga de Pollo
Tierna pechuga de pollo empanizada, servida con puré de papa, lechuga y jitomate.
O asada a la plancha acompañada de verduras salteadas.

Filete de Pescado
Fresco filete empanizado, servido con puré de papa y salsa tártara o preparado ricamente al mojo de ajo y servido con papas a la francesa.

● Choose a meal for:
  – someone on a diet.
  – a tourist who wants a typical Mexican meal.

● With a partner, practice ordering a meal you would like from this menu.

En el mercado

¡Vamos de compras al mercado!

There are markets in most towns and cities in Mexico. Selling food, flowers and household items, as well as handicrafts, markets are colorful and full of life.

Mexico City

Fonart (stores all over the city) The government sponsors these centers for handicrafts. Prices are fixed, but there is a degree of quality control.

Mercado de San Juan (Centro Artesanal, Calle Ayuntamiento and Aranda) This is a treasure house of stands and small shops, with merchandise piled high. This market is one of the most popular with visitors. There is bargaining here.

La Ciudadela (Calle Balderas and the Plaza Ciudadela) Articles from all over Mexico for sale here. There are workshops where you can watch things being made. You can bargain, too.

Centro de Antigüedades (Plaza del Angel, Calle de Londres 161) This market specializes in antiques. The shops are open all week, but the best day to go is Saturday.

Bazar Sábado (Plaza de San Jacinto 11, San Angel) San Angel is half an hour's drive from the city center, but the Bazar Sábado—on Saturdays only—is worth the drive. An old country house with a beautiful courtyard is the setting for shops selling paintings, handmade items and high-quality jewelry.

I'd like an antique vase for my mother . . .

Vamos al Centro de Antigüedades en la Zona Rosa.

. . . and a leather belt for my father.

Más tarde podemos ir al Bazar Sábado.

It's a bargain!

In markets you may be able to bargain over prices. Always be polite. If you really don't want something, say so. Don't waste the seller's time. Some traders may not want to bargain, but most of the craft items are still very good value.

If you are going to bargain, usually the seller gives you a price, you offer a lower one, then you discuss it and agree on a price somewhere in between.

Buenos días. ¿Cuánto cuesta el plato?

Para usted, un precio especial.

Es my bonito pero, ¿tiene usted platos más baratos?

Es el primer plato que he visto. Quiero ver los platos en otras tiendas.

Es precioso pero, ¿no puede darme un precio más bajo?

Bueno, señorita, le doy un precio especial, pero es el último precio.

Muy bien, señor.

Recuerdos de México

Buying presents is difficult—because there are so many things to choose from.

Traditional woven sandals or **huaraches**.

Botas de vaquero

Sombreros *are useful portable sunshades.*

Títeres

The hand-woven, woolen **sarapes** *range in size from child-size ponchos to bed covers.*

Traditional embroidered blouses and dresses.

Leather items such as **cinturones de piel**.

Also look for:
- glazed and painted pottery (**cerámica**).
- hand-woven shawls (**rebozos**).
- hand-woven baskets (**canastos**).
- silver jewelry (**joyería de plata**).
- silverware (**cubiertos**).
- metal work, especially copper (**artículos de cobre**).
- leather jackets and suitcases (**sacos y maletas de cuero**).
- lacquered wood (**madera barnizada**).
- glassware (**cristalería**).

¡Mira!

☞ Every region of Mexico has different craft items. This painting from the state of Guerrero is on **papel amate** (bark paper). What special items can you find?

Artesanías típicas

This craft market brochure has been translated into English, but someone has mixed up the explanations. Match each of the English translations with the Spanish original.

● How would you translate the opening hours into English?

¡Mira!

☞ In many food markets there is often an altar. Can you find one?

Barro negro, vistosa cerámica de fino acabado. Diseños tradicionales y modernos hechos en el poblado de San Bartolo Coyotepec.

Textiles tradicionales de lana y otros materiales, hechos en telar de cintura por indígenas Triquis (Mixteca).

Molinillos, cucharas y otros artículos de cocina tallados en madera.

Ropa típica, vestidos, huipiles, camisas y otras prendas tradicionales y modernas, con vistosos bordados.

Máscaras de diversos materiales, decorativas y ceremoniales.

**Abierto de lunes a sábado de 9:00 a 19:30 hrs.
Domingos de 9:00 a 13:00 hrs.**

A Ceremonial and decorative masks made from a variety of materials.

B Traditional woolen textiles and other items hand woven by Triqui (Mixtec) Indians.

C Attractive black-clay pottery, in modern and traditional designs, from San Bartolo Coyotepec.

D Hand-carved wooden beaters, spoons and other kitchen utensils.

E Typical clothing, dresses, huipiles, shirts and other traditional and modern clothes, with attractive embroidery.

41

At the stores

Puedes ir de compras también en tiendas, como los grandes almacenes. Aquí se paga el precio de etiqueta.

JEANS DE PANA VARIOS ESTILOS
PAGA PRECIO de ETIQUETA

Grandes Almacenes

These photos show different departments in a department store. Look at the store guide and see what floor each department is on. Remember that what is the first floor in Mexico is something different in the US.

¿Dónde hay ropa para jóvenes?

En el segundo piso.

①

DEPARTAMENTO	PISO
Cafetería	3
Dulces y pasteles	PB
Eléctricos	3
Fotografía	3
Juguetes	3
Ropa interior	2
Modas para caballero	1
Modas para dama	2
Para la cocina	3
Para la recámara	2
Perfumería	PB
Ropa para jóvenes	2
Ropa para niñas	2
Zapatos para caballero	1
Zapatos para dama	2

③

④

● What is the Spanish word for the cashier checkout?

La Zona Rosa

In the area bounded by **el Paseo de la Reforma**, **la Avenida Insurgentes**, **la Avenida Chapultepec** and **la calle de Florencia** lies **la Zona Rosa**. It came into being in the early 1950s as new shops opened up on streets west of the old city center. It was called **la Zona Dorada** and **la Zona Lila**, before the present name was settled on. Today it is full of elegant shops, art galleries, restaurants and discotheques.

● What does **la Zona Rosa** mean?
● What other colors were used to describe it?

Artículos de plata ▶

Un restaurante al aire libre

⑤

¿Cómo se dice?

There are a number of ways of asking for things you want to look at or try on in a store. With a partner, use the table below to practice asking to see or try the items shown.

Quiero	ver...
Quisiera	comprar...
Me gustaría	mirar...
Deseo	probarme...
¿Dónde podría	

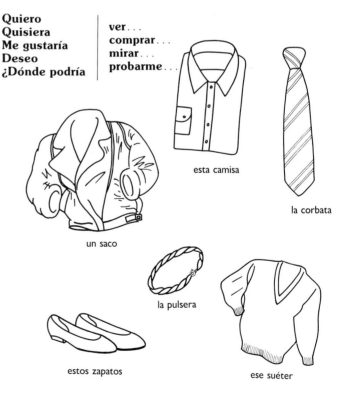

esta camisa

la corbata

un saco

la pulsera

estos zapatos

ese suéter

¿Sabes que...?

★ Stores are usually open from 9 or 10 am to 7 or 8 pm. In some places, they close for the 'lunch hour' between 2 and 4 pm.

Long distance travel

Por camión

Long-distance **camiones** (buses) are fast and efficient, especially if you travel on the deluxe service.
- What is the destination on this ticket?
- At what time does the bus leave?

MEXICO—ACAPULCO—ZIHUATANEJO

TRANSP. DE LUJO "LOS GALGOS"
S.A. DE C.V.

EVITE RECLAMACIONES, VERIFIQUE FECHA Y HORA DE SU SALIDA

AUTOBUSES DE ACAPULCO,
S.A. DE C.V.

Estrella de Oro, S.A. de C.V.

EN MEXICO:
TERMINAL CENTRAL DEL SUR
AV. TAXQUEÑA 1320
TEL. 549-85-20 CON 10 LINEAS
MEXICO 21. D.F.
EN ACAPULCO:
TERMINAL CENTRAL DE
AUTOBUSES DE PRIMERA CLASE
AV. CUAUHTEMOC 1490
TEL. 2-64-50 CON 5 LINEAS

No.

N$18.00

HORA: 18:30

DESTINO

Martes

CUERNAVACA

FECHA: 28 Julio

PASAJERO

ASIENTO: 33

EDUARDO DUARTE

There are many different bus companies. Here are some that run between Mexico City and other parts of the country:

Autobuses de Oriente Eastern Mexico, Veracruz, Puebla, Mérida and Cancún.

Estrella de Oro Deluxe service to Cuernavaca, Taxco and Acapulco.

Omnibus Cristóbal Colón Oaxaca, connections to Central America.

Omnibus de México Service north to Guadalajara, San Luis Potosí and El Paso.

Transportes Chihuahuenses Northern Mexico.

Transportes del Norte Monterrey and Matamoros.

Tres Estrellas de Oro Guadalajara, Mazatlán and Tijuana. Also Querétaro and Puerto Vallarta.

Before you put your baggage into the baggage compartment under the bus, get a ticket for it from the bus driver.

AVISO

SRES. PASAJEROS:
ANTES DE RETIRARSE DE LA VENTANILLA, REVISE HORA Y FECHA DE SUS BOLETOS - PARA EVITAR RECLAMACIONES POSTERIORES.

ATTE. LA GERENCIA

- What does this sign advise you to do before leaving the ticket counter?

AUTOBUSES DE ORIENTE

A.D.O. lo lleva a más de 130 ciudades dentro de los siguientes estados: Puebla, Veracruz, Tabasco, Campeche, Yucatán, Hidalgo, Oaxaca, Tamaulipas, Quintana Roo, Chiapas, y México, D.F. A.D.O. cuenta con los mejores autobuses del país para ofrecerle: seguridad, comodidad, puntualidad y cortesía. También transportamos sus envíos. Es por eso que hoy en día, A.D.O. es: EXPERIENCIA QUE HACE HISTORIA

TERMINALES EN MEXICO, D.F.

- How many states does this bus company serve?
- What other area that is not a state does it serve?
- What four things does A.D.O. offer its clients?

Por tren

Traveling by train on **Ferrocarriles Nacionales de México**, the Mexican national railroad company, you can go **primera** (first) or **segunda clase** (second class) on most routes.

The trains are sometimes named for the cities that they serve. For example, someone from Monterrey is **un regiomontano**, so the train that travels between Mexico City, Monterrey and the US-Mexican border is **el Regiomontano**.

- What do you think the Guadalajara to Mexico City train would be called? (See page 34.)

The Chihuahua Pacifico Railway runs from Chihuahua south to Los Mochis in the state of Sinaloa.

Por avión

The two national airlines are **Aeroméxico** and **Mexicana**. Aeroméxico's logo represents an Aztec warrior with an eagle headdress. Mexicana has a more stylized representation of an eagle in its logo.

Aeroméxico logo

Operará nuevos itinerarios y vuelos

Aumentará Aeroméxico, desde mañana, su oferta en rutas saturadas

Together, the two airlines serve 51 national destinations, as well as cities in the USA, Canada, Central and South America and Europe.
● Look at this headline. What will Aeroméxico do from tomorrow?

En la carretera

*To help motorists, the Ministry of Tourism operates a fleet of 224 green-and-white radio-controlled pickup trucks on all major highways. Mexicans call the patrolmen **los ángeles verdes**, because of the color of their trucks. The patrolmen speak English and offer mechanical assistance, first aid and information on highway conditions. This is all free of charge, except for gasoline, oil or spare parts.*

Roadside altars are erected everywhere in Mexico. Many are set up for religious reasons, some mark the site of road accidents.

Speed limits in towns and villages are often 30 km/h (**kilómetros por hora**) or less.

Signs with highway numbers and destinations are green.
● What is the number of this highway?
● What is the next city on this highway?

*Just like any other country, **infracciones** (tickets) are handed out for speeding or parking offenses and you have to pay **una multa** (a fine).*

Look out for signs with white symbols on a blue background which indicate places of interest. This one is for an archeological site at Yagul.
● Why is the symbol a pyramid?
● What other signs of this kind can you see? What places of interest are they for?

Bus and truck drivers like to give their buses and trucks **un apodo** (a nickname).
● What are the **apodos** for these buses?

You can tell where road vehicles come from by looking at their license plates. The plates carry an abbreviation of the name of the state where the vehicle was registered.
● Look at the names of states on pages 20 and 21 and figure out where these vehicles are from.
● If a license plate had Mex Mex on it, where would the vehicle be from?
● Have you seen any different license plates? What states were the vehicles from?

Town and country

I'd like to know about other places in Mexico. What about small towns?

Vamos a ver tres ciudades coloniales muy típicas, a saber . . .

Taxco

Taxco was already settled when the Spaniards arrived. After the Conquest, the first silver shipments to Spain came from mines in Taxco. Although the ore has run out, Taxco still has an association with silver. Its craftsmen are renowned for their skill in working silver—a trade which was introduced in 1929 by American William Spratling. The town is a national monument and no modern-style building is allowed.

In the 18th-century, French silver-mine owner, Don José de la Borda, made and spent several fortunes. With some of his wealth, he had the magnificent baroque church of Santa Prisca built. Borda said, "God gives to Borda; Borda gives to God."

Guanajuato

Guanajuato is another high-altitude silver mining town, standing at 6,700 feet (2,010 meters) above sea-level. It was founded in the mid-1500s when the Spaniards discovered silver there. The town is a pleasant jumble of narrow streets and old plazas.

In 1974 the first Cervantes Festival was held in Guanajuato. The festival began with open-air performances of short plays by Miguel de Cervantes (1547–1616). He was the Spanish novelist and playwright who wrote Don Quixote, *a novel about the adventures of a strange knight errant and his squire, Sancho Panza.*

Now participants from theatre groups around the world perform in venues like **el Teatro Juárez**. *Amateur groups still perform outdoors in the town plazas.*

3:30

9 FESTIVAL. Representaciones y eventos realizados durante el Festival Internacional Cervantino de Guanajuato. **Conjunto Acrobático Chino de Hebén.**

There is a legend that two lovers, who lived on the same street, were kept apart by their families. The couple was able to steal a kiss across the street because it was so narrow. Today, the street is called **el Callejón del Beso**. *Couples who kiss under the lovers' windows are guaranteed years of good luck.*

◄ This is information about the festival from a TV guide.
● What is the name of the festival in Spanish?
● What performing group is mentioned?
● What country is it from?

San Miguel de Allende

Another national monument is the town of San Miguel de Allende which stands at 6,070 feet (1,850 meters) above sea level. It was the scene of dramatic events in the War of Independence when Hidalgo's revolutionary followers joined forces with soldiers led by Ignacio Allende. The two leaders were later captured and shot. Allende's contribution to independence was commemorated in the change of his home town's name—from San Miguel el Grande to San Miguel de Allende.

● Why do you think these towns' names were changed?
  – Dolores Hidalgo (formerly Dolores)
  – Morelia (formerly Valladolid)

El Instituto Allende, *a fine arts school founded in 1938 by Stirling Dickinson, is the focal point for a community of artists, writers and craftsmen from Mexico and all over the world. Every year many students from North America come to study Spanish, fine arts and local crafts.*

*Picture postcards from Europe are said to have inspired Ceferino Gutiérrez, the builder of a well-known landmark, **la Parroquia**. The parish church façade was built in the Gothic style, based on designs that the uneducated mason had drawn with a stick on the ground.*

En el campo

Under the land reform laws of the 1915 Constitution, many large **haciendas** (farms) were broken up and the land distributed. Title to tracts of land was given to **ejidos**, groups of **campesinos** (peasant farmers). Plots of land could be passed on from father to child, but could not be bought, sold or rented. The limited size of smallholdings often allowed farmers to grow just enough corn, beans and vegetables for their families to live on. It was not easy for them to improve their farming efficiency.

A new law in 1992 ended the state protection of **ejidos**, permitting **ejidatarios** (holders of **ejidos**) to sell or rent their land and introducing other measures to modernize the agricultural sector.

*Many hundreds of cacti and succulents exist in Mexico. Over the centuries people have learned how useful these plants can be. **El nopal** is a food source. Once the spines have been removed from the fruit, **la tuna** (prickly pear), it can be eaten. The leaves are cooked and eaten in stews or in salads.*

En el campo

Vacation time

México
Major Beaches and Resorts

Mexico has 4,438 miles (7,140 km) of coastline along **el Océano Pacífico** and **el Mar de Cortés** and 1,774 miles (2,854 km) along **el Golfo de México** and **el Mar Caribe**. In the south, jungle-covered hills come right down to the palm-fringed beaches. On the Caribbean coast there are many beaches of powder-white sand.

● How would you say 'the Atlantic Ocean' in Spanish?

When Mexicans go on organized tours to beach resorts, they can choose from **viajes todo pagado (VTP)** (all-inclusive package) or **viajes hotel incluido (VHI)** (transportation and hotel paid but no meals included). Look at these two ads for vacation packages.

● What does the **VHI** package include?
● What does Mexicana offer in its **VTP**?

 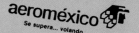

On the Pacific coast

Acapulco is often thought of as a resort for foreign tourists, but many Mexicans also spend their vacations there. They often stay in vacation homes, rather than hotels. **La semana santa**, the week before Easter, is a favorite vacation time for Mexicans, as is the summer.

Founded in 1850, Puerto Vallarta was a small fishing village until the American movie *The Night of the Iguana* was filmed there in 1964. Movie stars, like Elizabeth Taylor and Richard Burton, bought houses there, and other tourists came to enjoy the village's spectacular setting on the 28-mile (45 km) bay, **la Bahía de Banderas**. Puerto Vallarta has a marina and is also a port of call for

cruise ships. After extensive studies, the neighboring villages of Ixtapa and Zihuatanejo, just north of Acapulco, were chosen by the Mexican government for development into a new tourist resort. The area's natural assets of year-round good weather and scenic beauty were transformed into Ixtapa, a modern resort with the bonus of Zihuatanejo, an attractive old town.

The cliff divers of Acapulco are famous. From the top of La Quebrada, they dive 136 feet (41.5 meters) to the shallow inlet below. To make sure there is enough water, the dive must be timed so that the moment the diver enters the water coincides with an extra large wave pouring into the inlet.

El malecón, a palm-lined oceanside walk, is popular with visitors for afternoon and evening strolls.

Ixtapa has 14 beaches and many new hotels, as well as a golf course and a yacht marina. Along the coast, visitors can see turtles and pelicans.

Sea of Cortés and Baja California

As well as being a resort, Mazatlán is a major port city and the home of a large commercial fishing fleet.

Baja California, with its desert scenery, cliff formations and mountains, has a number of vacation spots—Ensenada, San Felipe and La Paz.

The Caribbean

Some buildings in Cancún are still roofed with traditional thatch.

Much of the Yucatán coast is limestone. Over the centuries, the pounding of the Caribbean waves has crushed the limestone into snow-white sand. Mexico's Caribbean coast is known as **la costa turquesa**, because of the vivid color of the water.

Located on a lagoon, fringed with wild jungle, is the resort of Cancún. Computer analysis showed the area to be an ideal location for tourism. In the 1960s, a completely new resort, with facilities such as roads, electricity, a telephone system, hotels and an airport, was carved out of the jungle.

Off the coast are two islands, Isla Mujeres and Cozumel, which developed as resorts when divers came to visit the coral reefs.

◄ *The region is especially popular with sports fishermen who fish for species like* **marlín, pez vela** *(sailfish), and* **atún** *(tuna).*

¡Vamos a la playa!

¡Me encanta ir a la playa! Todos los veranos voy a la costa con mi familia.

Is there much to do at beach resorts?

¡Sí, hay muchas cosas que hacer . . .!

¿Qué te gusta hacer en la playa?

. . . broncearme.

. . . correr las olas.

. . . lanzar en paracaídas.

. . . montar a caballo.

. . . correr.

. . . el buceo.

. . . el esquí acuático.

Me gusta el paracaídas.

A mí, me gusta broncearme.

. . . el windsurfing.

● With a partner, practice saying what you like to do at the beach.

En la Costa Norte

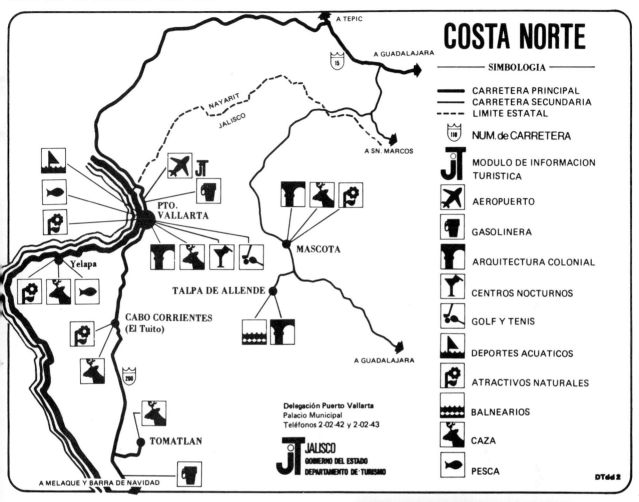

This tourist map shows Puerto Vallarta and its surrounding area with all the activities that are available to tourists.
- Where would you suggest someone interested in fishing and a quiet time should go?
- Would you find an airport at Talpa de Allende?
- Which highway runs north towards Puerto Vallarta?
- Which town is the tourist information office in?
- Which place would you like to stay in? What facilities does it offer?

- What kind of service is being offered on this sign?
- How can you save money?

◄ This sticker is encouraging people in Puerto Vallarta to do something.
- What is it?

Free time

¿Qué hacemos en las horas libres?

Ir al cine

Ir al cine (going to the movies) is a popular way of spending the evening. Mexico produces many **películas** (films) and **telenovelas** (soaps) which are seen in movie theaters and on television throughout Latin America. Many films from the USA are dubbed into Spanish.

- Look at this ad for a new movie theater, Polanco I and II.
  1 What is the Spanish word for movie theater?
  2 What does the ad promise about the screens and the sound?

RECOMENDA-CION

★★★★
EXCELENTE

★★★
BUENA

★★
REGULAR

★
MALA

La Orilla de la Tierra

México
★★★

9 FANTASIA Hasta un pueblo alejado de todas partes llega un hombre a hablar de la existencia de un gran tesoro, los hombres del pueblo van en su busca y abandonan a las mujeres. Más tarde, llega una peregrinación y las mujeres abandonan el lugar. En el pueblo, sólo queda una adolescente que espera a que llegue un arcángel por ella.

Arcadia Plus
Balderas 36, 521 76 16.
11:00, 12:50, 14:40, 16:30, 18:20, 20:10 horas

Variedades 1 Plus
Av. Juárez 58 y Luis Moya, Centro, 521-7835.
11:00, 12:40, 14:20, 16:00, 17:40, 19:20, 21:00 horas.

- This film features a village so far away from anywhere that it seems to be on the edge of the world. Answer the questions that these movie goers have about the film.
  1 What is the movie called?
  2 In which movie theater can I see a show around seven o'clock in the evening?
  3 In the movie, why do all the men leave the village?
  4 Who is the only person left in the village?
  5 Is it a good film?

*Movie star Cantinflas was well loved by all Mexicans. His real name was Mario Moreno, but he became known as Cantinflas after playing the part of a Mexico City tramp in several comedy films, including **Los tres mosqueteros** and **Soy un prófugo**. Movie audiences around the world got to know him for his role as Passepartout, valet to Phileas Fogg, in* Around the World in 80 days.

- Here are two **películas** which are both **dibujos animados** (cartoons). How would you say the titles in English?

Viendo la televisión

La red nacional (national network) has seven television **canales** (channels). All **canales** are private, except **Canal 11** which is owned by the state television company, Imevisión. The other television stations are **Canal 2, 4, 5, 7, 9** and **13**.

Mexico City has **Canal 22**, a special channel with a variety of **emisiones** (programs) on cultural and scientific themes. There are also other regional channels for different parts of Mexico.

*Information about **emisiones** is given in **periódicos** (newspapers) and TV guides like **Tele Guía**.*

¿Qué tipo de programa es?

- Here is a list of the different kinds of **programas** (programs) that you might see on **la televisión** (television). What kind of **programas** are they?
  - a **Las películas**
  - b **Los reportajes**
  - c **Los documentales**
  - d **Las telenovelas**
  - e **Los dibujos animados**
  - f **Los deportes**
  - g **Los concursos**
  - h **Las aventuras policiacas**
  - g **Los noticiarios**

> **2 AGUJETAS DE COLOR DE ROSA.** Telenovela. Capítulos 309 y 310.
> **7 ¡EXPRESATE!** Debates juveniles a temas de interés general.
> **5 PRIMER IMPACTO.** Reportajes periodísticos.
> **2 ¡LLEVATELO!** Concursos para toda la familia.
> **11 EL INVESTIGADOR.**
>
> Aventuras policiacas.
> **13 NOTICIARIO HECHOS.**
> **4 FUTBOL SOCCER NACIONAL.** Campeonato de Liga. Directo desde el Estadio Azteca, en Tlalpan, Distrito Federal. "LAS AGUILAS" DEL AMERICA vs. "LA FRANJA" DEL PUEBLA.
> **9 LA PANTERA ROSA.** Dibujos animados.

- Look at this selection of **programas** from different channels on Mexican television. What program would you suggest for:
  - a a soccer fan from Puebla who can't go to Mexico City?
  - b a family that likes watching game shows together?
  - c someone who wants to know what is happening in the news?
  - d a soap fan?

Mi programa favorito se llama "¡Exprésate!".

- Some other television viewers watch **¡Exprésate!** and have written to say how much they like it.
  1 How old are the television viewers?
  2 How many of them have signed the letter?
  3 What Spanish word do they use to say how good the program is?
  4 What part of Mexico do they live in?

> Somos un grupo de jóvenes entre 15 y 17 años que seguimos los nuevos programas de diversión que han hecho para nosotros. Nos fascina en particular esa emisión "¡Exprésate!" donde se tratan temas y problemas de los jóvenes de nuestra edad. ¡Fenomenal! ¡Al fin se acordaron de nosotros!
>
> **Adriana Llerena López, Gabriela Armenta Velasco (y 25 firmas más), Paseo Jardinera 109, México, D.F.**

- With a partner, practice saying which is your favorite kind of TV program.

¿Qué tipo de programa te gusta?

Prefiero las telenovelas.

Me gustan más los deportes.

Musical matters

Los mariachis

Mariachi music is what most visitors think of as typically Mexican. The name **mariachi** is said to have come from the French word 'mariage' (wedding). **La música ranchera** is another name for this type of music. During the French occupation of Mexico in the 1860s, the French heard bands and thought they were playing for weddings.

The players and singers are always men. In the traditional dress of **charro** horsemen, they play violins, double bass, trumpets and trombones. The songs are often sad, telling of lost or unrequited love.

One of the top mariachi stars is Vicente Fernández, who comes from the State of Jalisco. He has toured Latin America and southwestern USA. As well as having 15 number one hits, he has appeared in many musical films.

*Guadalajara is considered to be the home of mariachi music. Located in the city center is **la Plaza de los Mariachis**.*

*In Mexico City you can visit **la Plaza Garibaldi** (see above) and see the mariachi musicians play. Some wait there to be hired for a party. Others are hired by romantic husbands or boyfriends to serenade their wives or girlfriends. Occasionally the husband or boyfriend may even sing himself. Onlookers never applaud or comment, because it is really a private serenade that they are being allowed to listen to.*

***La marimba** is a kind of xylophone. Sometimes several performers play together at the same time. You may see groups of marimba players performing in the street.*

¡Mira!

☞ Watch for groups of **concheros** giving performances in the Zócalo in Mexico City or in main squares in other towns. They perform pre-Columbian dances in the costumes of the time.

El Ballet Folklórico

Every July **La Guelaguetza** festival is held in Oaxaca. People gather from all over the state and dance their traditional dances. A group from **el Ballet Folklórico** (above) dances **un jarabe**, a dance from Jalisco.

In 1952, prima ballerina and choreographer Amalia Hernández founded **el Ballet Folklórico de México**. By presenting folk dances from all over Mexico, the ballet has helped to safeguard centuries-old traditional music and dance. Mexican history, especially the Revolution, is also portrayed in dance.

Since then **el Ballet Folklórico** has expanded into five companies and a school, and given over 4,000 performances in locations ranging from tents in small Mexican villages to the world's most famous theatres.

This restaurant in the Zona Rosa has traditional entertainment.
- What night is the show?
- What is the Spanish word for 'atmosphere'?
- What three kinds of musical entertainment are offered?

Vamos también a bailar a la discoteca.

- What day will this dance take place?
- What groups will be playing?

Sport

El futbol

Soccer (**el futbol**) is the most popular sport in Mexico. There is a soccer league with three divisions. The First Division has 20 teams from all over the country—five come from Mexico City and four from Guadalajara. Other large cities have one or two teams each.

One of the biggest games of the year is between **América** and **Guadalajara** who are rival teams from Mexico City and Guadalajara.

América venció a Neza 3 a 1

Another Mexico City soccer team is **Nezahualcóyotl**, called **Neza** for short. The newspaper headline gives the score from a game between **América** and **Neza**.
- Who won the game and what was the scoreline?

Mexico has twice hosted **el Mundial**, the soccer World Cup competition, once in 1970 and again in 1986. Unfortunately, Mexico has never won **el Mundial**, although it has often qualified for the finals. Argentina, Brazil and Uruguay have all won the World Cup.

During the 1986 **Mundial** a total of nearly a million people came to watch games in **el Estadio Azteca** (Aztec Stadium) in Mexico City. Other games were played in Guadalajara, León, Monterrey, Puebla and Querétaro.

When **la selección nacional** (Mexican national team) plays, the players wear green shirts, white shorts and red socks.

Another kind of soccer which is popular is **el futbolín** which is played in cafés all over Mexico.

¿Cómo se dice?

Match the logos with the sports.

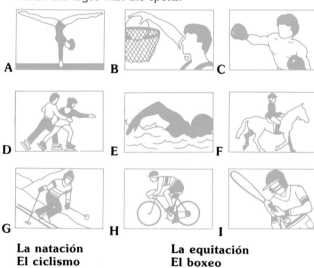

La natación
El ciclismo
La gimnástica
El básquetbol
El esquí

La equitación
El boxeo
El patinaje
El béisbol

- With a partner, say what your favorite sport is.

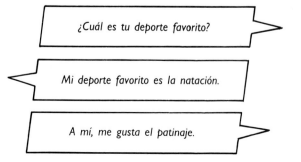

¿Cuál es tu deporte favorito?

Mi deporte favorito es la natación.

A mí, me gusta el patinaje.

Otros deportes

The tradition of **la corrida de toros** came originally from Spain. Mexico has bullfighters of its own and others visit from Spain. **La corrida** takes place at **la plaza de toros** and starts at 4 or 5pm. During the afternoon, there are usually three **toreros** who will each fight two bulls. The principal **plaza de toros** in Mexico City is **la Arena México** which holds about 30,000 people.

● Where is this bullfight to take place?
● This bullfight commemorates the founding of Mérida. How many years ago was it founded?

◄ ● What kind of sport is this competition poster for?
Can both men and women enter?
● What date does it start on?

From the north comes **la charreada**. **Los charros** (the riders) are often amateurs. Dressed in elegant **charro** suits they show off their skills in roping steers and horses, and bronco busting.

● Look up the words **rodeo** and **bronco** in an English dictionary. What are the origins of these words?

4 FUTBOL AMERICANO PROFESIONAL. N.F.L. Temporada **"PARTIDO ESPECIAL DE DIA DE GRACIA".** Directo desde los Estados Unidos, en el Texas Stadium: "EMPACADORES" DE GREEN BAY vs. "VAQUEROS" DE DALLAS. Comentarios: Antonio de Valdés, José Segarra, Enrique Burak.

4 BEISBOL DE LAS GRANDES LIGAS. Directo desde los Estados Unidos. Opciones. CALIFORNIA vs. BALTIMORE o CINCINNATI vs. CHICAGO W.B.S. Comentarios: Antonio de Valdés, Pedro "Mago" Septién, Jorge "Sonny" Alarcón.

El béisbol and **el futbol americano** are also popular. Look at these TV listings.

● Are these programs broadcast live from the United States?
● Which football teams are playing?
● The football game takes place on a special day. What is it?
● There are two possible baseball games. What are they?

LOS ANGELES NEGROS DE PUEBLA

LOS DIABLOS ROJOS DE MEXICO

LOS TIGRES DE MEXICO

LOS LEONES DE YUCATAN

● Here are some teams from **la Liga Mexicana de Béisbol**. What are their names in English?

¿Sabes que . . . ?

★ A number of Mexicans play professional baseball in the USA.

Keeping in touch with home

¡Mándame una postal!

Everyone at home loves to get post-cards. You can buy **tarjetas postales** (often just called **postales**) in your hotel or in other stores. It's surprising how much information you can squeeze into a small space.

Cuando fui de vacaciones a Acapulco, envié una postal a mi amiga María.

Querida María,
Llegamos aquí ayer por la noche.
¡Es precioso! El hotel tiene dos albercas. ¡Hace mucho calor en la playa!
Ana

● When did Ana arrive?
● What does she like about the hotel?

If you want to write a letter home, buy *papel y sobres para correo aéreo*. The paper and envelopes are made especially light so that even long letters aren't too expensive to mail.

¿Cómo se dice?

Perdone usted, señor. ¿Dónde está el correo?

Aquí mismo, detrás de usted.

Buenos días. Dos estampillas para postales a los Estados Unidos, por favor.

¿Por correo aéreo o por vía terrestre?

Por vía aérea.

¿Dónde las echo al correo?

Allá en el buzón.

● If you are mailing a card home, which slot would you put it in?
● Where would a letter be going if it is in the middle slot?
● How would you say 'surface mail' in Spanish?

If you already have stamps for your cards and letters and need a mail box, look for one of these...

¿Sabes que...?

★ Post offices are open from 8 am to 6 pm on weekdays and from 9 am to 1 pm on Saturdays and Sundays.

¡Mira!

☞ It's worth buying a stamp at **el Correo Mayor** in Mexico City just for the architecture. The interior is an impressive combination of wrought iron, marble, crystal fixtures and mosaics.

Una llamada por teléfono

◄ **Cabinas telefónicas** (telephone booths) for local calls are found in convenient places in Mexican towns and cities. To make your **llamada** (call) you can use **monedas** (coins) or **una tarjeta de teléfono** (a prepaid phone card).

In Mexico City the location of a telephone booth is often indicated by a sign at a street intersection. You may find this useful if you make a call, because you will know what street you are on.

¿Cómo se dice?

 Esperar el tono

Marcar el número

 *No contesta el número*

Está ocupado

 Colgar

Llamadas a larga distancia

You can make long distance calls from your hotel or from a long-distance telephone booth (**una caseta de larga distancia**). Calls from **una caseta de larga distancia** may be cheaper than from your hotel, because hotels put an extra charge on phone calls. Because government taxes make international calls from Mexico very expensive, it is often cheaper to call collect. If you do call collect, you have to go through an operator which can mean long delays.

¿Sabes que...?

★ If you're on a summer vacation in Mexico, US daylight savings can mean that the eastern US will be two hours ahead of most parts of Mexico, three hours ahead of resorts like La Paz or Puerto Vallarta, and four hours ahead of Tijuana or Mexicali.

Lada 95

Larga distancia automática a Estados Unidos y Canadá de teléfono a teléfono

Ejemplo de marcación:

95	+	713	+	Número Deseado
Acceso al Sistema Lada Internacional de Teléfono a Teléfono		Clave de Area de Houston, Tex.		Teléfono en Houston, Tex.

- Invariablemente se tendrán que marcar 12 dígitos.
- Después de marcar, espere un tiempo razonable hasta que se establezca su comunicación. No cuelgue antes de tiempo, espere a recibir algún tono.
- En llamadas internacionales es necesario esperar, algunas veces hasta 45 segundos.

- La conferencia se contabiliza en el momento en que contestan. Si el teléfono está ocupado o no contestan, la llamada no se cobra.
- El costo mínimo por conferencia es de un minuto de teléfono a teléfono.

These instructions in the phone book tell you how to dial the USA and Canada.

- What number do you dial for access to the international long distance network?

- How do you say 'area code' in Spanish?
- How many digits must you dial?
- Do you pay for the call if no one answers?
- Is there a minimum charge for a call?

Help!

> Even on the best organised trip, problems may arise from time to time.

¡Me perdí!

> M-á-s d-e-s-p-a-c-i-o, p-o-r f-a-v-o-r.

In a strange city you may get lost if you get separated from your friends. Write down the name and address of your hotel and always carry it with you. It is much easier to ask for directions if you can show the address.

If you don't understand the directions that someone gives you in Spanish the first time, don't panic. Say politely **otra vez más despacio, por favor** (say it again slowly, please) and the person should repeat the instructions for you.

VIADUCTO
DELEGACION BENITO JUAREZ   Z.P. 12

FCO. I. MADERO
Delegación CUAUHTEMOC   Z.

Find out where you are by looking for a sign with the name of the street you are on. Look at a street map to familiarize yourself with the names of the main streets and the district of the town or city where you are staying.

In Mexico City, street intersection signs also give the name of the district.

● What districts are these streets in?

You may be unlucky enough to lose something. Report the loss of anything valuable to the police as soon as possible. Get a copy of the police report to send on to your insurance company when you make a claim. Your hotel may be able to help you with this.

> ¿Qué ha perdido usted?

He perdido...

los lentes de contacto

el dinero

la cartera

los anteojos de sol

el pasaporte

la cámara

los cheques de viajero

el boleto de avión

● With a partner, explain what item(s) you have lost.

Sometimes, through a misunderstanding you may find yourself in an embarrassing situation. As well as a friendly smile, there are two words that can be very useful.

> ¡Perdón!

> ¡Disculpe!

No me siento muy bien

Most hotels have a doctor on call day or night, so if you have a problem, ask the reception desk to contact **el doctor** or **el médico**. If you want to be sure of finding a doctor or dentist who speaks English, telephone your embassy or consulate, or one of the major hotels.

You will have to pay for the doctor's services. Be sure to ask for **un recibo**, a receipt which you can use to make a claim on your medical insurance.

The doctor will probably give you **una receta** (prescription) to take to **la farmacia**. Remember to ask for **un recibo** for the medicine. If you need medicine at night, ask for **la farmacia de guardia**.

● What is the Spanish word for 'ambulance'?

¿Cómo se dice?

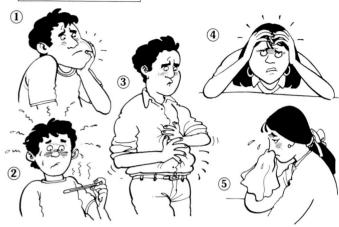

You may have to explain a medical problem to a chemist or a doctor. Match each caption with the correct picture.

A **Tengo un resfriado.**
B **Tengo dolor de cabeza.**
C **Me duele una muela.**
D **Tengo fiebre.**
E **Tengo dolor de estómago.**

● What should you do in case of fire?

¡Mira!

☞ When you stand at street intersections, look at the signs. A pedestrian crossing is a yellow sign. What other signs like this can you see? Can you find out what **delegación** you're in?

Teléfonos de emergencia

LOCATEL Servicio de información y ayuda sobre personas y vehículos extraviados, urgencias médicas, crisis emocionales, servicios públicos diversos. Tel. 658 1111.
CENTRO ANTIRRABICO Tel. 549 4293.
CRUZ ROJA Tel. 557 57 57.
PATRULLAS DE AUXILIO TURÍSTICO EN CARRETERAS Tels. 250 8221, 250 8555 ext. 130 y 297.
POLICÍA Tel. 588 5100.
POLICÍA DE CAMINOS Tel. 684 2142.

Here is a list of phone numbers that may be useful in an emergency.
● Locatel can give information on various problems. Describe three things you could ask Locatel for information on.
● What problem might you have if you were calling 250 8555?

Concurso

Try this quiz to see how much you know about Mexico now. All the information you need is in the book.

1 Which of these outlines is Mexico?

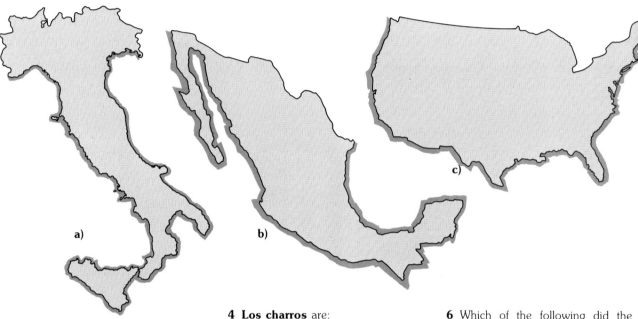

a)

b)

c)

2 Una torta is:
a) a sandwich.
b) a turtle.
c) an apple pie.

3 Why do an eagle and a snake appear on Mexican coins?

4 Los charros are:
a) musicians.
b) truck drivers.
c) horsemen.

5 Which famous Mexican painter and muralist came from Guadalajara?

6 Which of the following did the Spanish bring to Mexico?
a) Horses.
b) Corn.
c) Chocolate.
d) Grapes.
e) Cows.
f) Tobacco.
g) Tomatoes.

7 Una tuna is:
a) a fish.
b) a prickly pear.
c) a flower.

8 The people who built Tenochtitlán were called:
a) the Mayas.
b) the Aztecs.
c) the Toltecs.
d) the Mixtecs.

9 The holiday resort of Acapulco is:
a) on the Caribbean coast.
b) in the State of Guerrero.
c) in Baja California.
d) in the Yucatán Peninsula.

10 What is a back yard called in Mexico?

11 **Tierra y Libertad** was the rallying cry for which of the leaders of the 1910 Revolution?
  a) Francisco Madero.
  b) Emiliano Zapata.
  c) Pancho Villa.

12 How do you say 'enjoy your meal' in Spanish?
  a) **Buenas tardes.**
  b) **¡Qué rico!**
  c) **¡Buen provecho!**

13 President Benito Juárez was:
  a) a Zapotec.
  b) an Olmec.
  c) an Aztec.

14 What kind of transport is available where you see this sign?

15 What job does **un mesero** do?
  a) Collects refuse.
  b) Waits on tables.
  c) Works in a mine.

16 Quetzalcóatl is:
  a) a feathered snake god.
  b) the capital of Tlaxcala State.
  c) a soccer team.

17 What is the Spanish name for this kind of store?

18 The world's largest city park is in Mexico City and is called:
  a) Alameda.
  b) Zócalo.
  c) Chapultepec.

19 This statue is in the Plaza Garibaldi. What kind of music would this musician play?

20 Which of these can you buy as souvenirs to bring back from Mexico?
  a) **Huaraches.**
  b) **Sombreros.**
  c) **Charreadas.**
  d) **Sarapes.**
  e) **Botas de vaquero.**
  f) **Conquistadores.**
  g) **Joyería de plata.**
  h) **Pescadores.**

21 What are these sports called in Spanish?

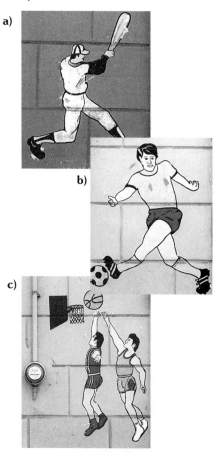

Answers on page 80

Ahora vamos a ver los otros países de Centroamérica y de América del Sur. Para recordar los nombres de estos países, véase la página 4. ¿Listos? ¡Vamos!

Mountains, jungle and deserts

Una diversidad geográfica

The Spanish-speaking countries of Central and South America cover an area, stretching from the tropical area on the Mexican-Guatemalan border to the barren, windswept **Cabo de Hornos** (Cape Horn) at the southern tip of Chile. Ecuador is on **el Ecuador** (Equator), while **el Cabo de Hornos** is 600 miles (965 km) from Antarctica.

The three main kinds of terrain are:

☐ **La costa:** In Central America, Ecuador and Colombia the coast is tropical. Further south in Peru and northern Chile, it changes into desert.

☐ **La sierra:** The Andes chain runs from Panama to Cape Horn.

☐ **La selva:** Tropical rain forest and jungles extend along the banks of the world's second longest river, the Amazon. There are also large areas of tropical rain forest in Central America.

Most people think of equatorial areas as hot, but it is possible to feel cold standing at the Equator line. The temperature drops approximately 1°F for every 300 feet of altitude. Where the Equator passes through the Andes near Quito, the capital of Ecuador, at 7,789 feet (2,374 meters), the temperature can drop very low. Only at sea level and in low-lying areas do you find the kind of steamy heat usually associated with the Equator.

The Andes mountain chain stretches 4,500 miles (7,242 km) from Central America down into South America. It includes some of the world's highest peaks:

Chimborazo: 20,702 feet (6,310 meters). An extinct **volcán** (volcano) and the highest peak in Ecuador, it was once thought to be the highest mountain in the world. Cotopaxi at 19,457 feet (5,895 meters) is the highest active volcano in the world. This area where there are many volcanoes is known as **la Avenida de los volcanes**.

Huascarán: 22,205 feet (6,768 meters). This is the highest mountain in Peru. In the same area, **el Callejón de Huaylas**, there are 10 peaks over 20,000 feet (6,096 meters). Although the mountains are within the tropics, they are snow-capped and have glaciers. The glacial lakes are strikingly beautiful.

Illimani: 21,004 feet (6,402 meters). The mountain dominates La Paz in Bolivia, the world's highest capital at 11,929 feet (3,636 meters) above sea level. It was built in a canyon 1,214 feet (370 meters) below the level of **el Altiplano**, a vast plain in the middle of the Andes. Most of **el Altiplano** is above 13,000 feet (3,963 meters). Nearly 70 percent of Bolivia's 6.3 million population lives on this stark, treeless plain. The airport for La Paz, **el Alto**, is up on **el Altiplano** and is the highest commercial airport in the world.

El cerro de Cotopaxi

El cerro de Illimani

Aconcagua: 22,834 feet (6,960 meters). In the southern section of the Andes which separates Chile and Argentina is Aconcagua, the highest peak in the Americas.

Chile is one of the smallest South American countries. Although it is 2,610 miles (4,200 km) long, on average it measures only 112 miles (180 km) across. Neighboring Argentina is the second largest country in South America after Brazil.

*Some of the driest areas of the world are found in South America. This happens because winds moving towards the Pacific coast are cooled as they blow over cold ocean currents and carry very little moisture. The coast of Peru is mostly desert, with occasional green oases. In northern Chile, in some parts of **el desierto de Atacama** (Atacama Desert), no rainfall has ever been recorded.*

La cuenca amazónica

The total area drained by **la cuenca amazónica** (Amazon Basin) — 2.3 million square miles (5.8 million square km) —is nearly two-thirds of the size of the USA. The jungle of **la cuenca amazónica** is usually associated with Brazil, but it extends into many other countries. Colombia, Ecuador, Peru and Bolivia, often thought of as mainly mountainous, all have vast rain forests. About 40 percent of Venezuela is rain forest.

The first recorded journey along **el río Amazonas** was by Spanish conquistador Francisco de Orellana. He was a member of an expedition looking for gold that set off from Guayaquil (now in modern Ecuador) and crossed the Andes. Many of the expedition's members fell sick or died. Orellana and a small group set off by boat down the Coca river to look for food.

Orellana never came back. Instead he followed the Coca until it joined a larger river, the Amazon. Eight months later, he and his crew reached the Atlantic Ocean after a journey of nearly 4,000 miles. In their small ship, they sailed on up the Atlantic coast to Trinidad and then across the Atlantic to Spain, where few people believed their story.

The river became known as the Amazon, because one of the tribes that attacked Francisco de Orellana's group had women fighting alongside the men. This recalled the Amazons, who were women warriors of Ancient Greek legend.

La historia natural

Yo soy amiga de la naturaleza. ¿Y tú?

Llamas, alpacas and **vicuñas** are all from the camel family. Their warm coats help them to survive at high altitudes. **Llamas** and **alpacas** are kept for meat and wool and for use as pack animals. **La vicuña** is valued for its silky wool.

El cóndor is an important symbol in Andean folklore and condor designs are often woven into cloaks. It is a rare vulture, found in the Andes.

El quetzal lives in the rain forests of Central America, feeding on fruit, insects, tree frogs and lizards. The male has vivid green, red and white plumage. It is now rare.

This is an ad for a job in the Amazon area of Ecuador.
● What kind of job is it? Is it job temporary or permanent?
● What kind of experience must applicants have?

Six hundred miles off the coast of Ecuador is **el Archipiélago de Colón** (Galapagos Islands), consisting of 12 main islands and other smaller ones. The islands became well known after the visit of naturalist Charles Darwin in 1835. He observed that many of the species on the islands were unique, having evolved in a completely different way from species on the South American mainland. Today, the Ecuadorian government has made the islands into a nature reserve. Only limited numbers of tourists are allowed to come and observe creatures like the giant Galapagos tortoise (above) or Darwin's finches.

Sea, land and skyways

El Canal de Panamá

The 50-mile (80 km) Panama Canal took 32 years to build. Excavation was started in 1882 under Ferdinand de Lesseps, builder of the Suez Canal. Defeated by tropical diseases such as malaria and yellow fever, and by financial problems, the company building the canal went bankrupt in 1889.

Only in 1903 did work start again when the USA acquired rights to finish the canal. US Army Colonel William C. Gorgas played an important part in making the building work less deadly by eliminating the mosquitoes that carried malaria and yellow fever. On August 15, 1914, the first ship passed through the canal. Using the canal cuts 7,873 miles (12,676 km) off the sea journey from New York to San Francisco.

Under the 1903 treaty the USA established a canal zone over which it had sovereignty. The zone extended five miles (eight km) on each side of the canal and included the cities of Cristóbal and Balboa. This treaty was renegotiated in 1978 and it was agreed that control of the canal will pass to Panama in the year 2000.

¿Sabes que...?

★ Panama was not the only place considered as a canal site. The other sites proposed were:
  ☐ in southern Nicaragua, using access across Lake Nicaragua and down the San Juan river to the Atlantic Ocean.
  ☐ across the Tehuantepec Isthmus in southern Mexico.
  ☐ across northern Colombia near the Colombian-Panamanian border.

  Find these areas in an atlas and look at where they are in relation to Panama.
  ☐ At 11,410 feet (3,478 meters) on the summit of **el volcán Baru** in northern Panama you can see the Pacific Ocean and the Caribbean Sea.

Por vía ferroviaria

The railroads played a major role in opening up South America in the 19th century. The main period of expansion, between the 1850s and the 1930s, was largely financed by US, British and French companies, which also designed and constructed many of the railroads.

The railroad networks were aimed more at serving the economic needs of the foreign investors than those of the people living in countries like Argentina, Chile, Peru and Bolivia. Railroads would move grain, meat, wool and minerals from the interior to the ports for shipment to the US or to Europe.

Building railroads in the Andes required great engineering skills. Many tunnels and bridges had to be built. In Peru, the Huancayo railroad has 16 switchbacks to allow trains to climb up the mountain. The line's highest point is the Ticlio tunnel at 15,610 feet (4,758 meters) above sea level.

La Zona Andina nos sorprende con la majestuosidad del Tren a las Nubes. Con un recorrido de 219 kms, desde Salta, ciudad capital, ubicada a 1.187 m.s.n.m. se llega hasta el viaducto La Polvorilla, a 4.200 m.s.n.m. El Tren a las Nubes, producto de la capacidad profesional del Ing. Ricardo Fontaine Maury, es una impresionante obra de ingeniería ferroviaria. El tren atraviesa 29 puentes, 21 túneles y 13 viaductos.

Read the extract from a brochure about **el Tren a las Nubes** which runs in the north of Argentina.
- Why do you think this train is called **el Tren a las Nubes**?
- What is the abbreviation for the Spanish words **metros sobre el nivel del mar** (meters above sea level)?
- What was the name of the engineer in charge of building the railroad?
- Are there more tunnels than bridges and viaducts on the line?

La carretera panamericana

At a congress in 1923 the American nations decided to build a highway that would link the capitals of their countries — north and south. Later the plans were altered so that some capitals are linked up by connecting roads.

La carretera panamericana (Pan-American Highway), as it became known, runs over 17,000 miles (27,350 km) — the full length of the Americas from Fairbanks, Alaska to Punta Arenas in Chile. The only break is at the Darien Gap in Panama. The Panamanians call the gap **el Tapón** (the stopper). The difficulties of the terrain and environmental concerns have so far prevented completion of this 250-mile (402-km) stretch.

After the highway crosses the US-Mexican border at Nuevo Laredo, the first capital is Mexico City. Once in South America, the route of **la carretera panamericana** goes down the west coast of South America, linking Bogotá in Colombia, Lima in

La carretera panamericana en el Perú

Peru and Santiago, the capital of Chile. From Chile **la carretera panamericana** crosses the Andes to Argentina and across the plains to the Argentinian capital, Buenos Aires. Connecting roads link up other capitals.

● Look at a map of the Americas. When **la carretera panamericana** crosses the southern border of Mexico, what six Central American capitals does the road pass through?

Pioneros de los cielos

The early days of air transportation in Central and South America in the 1920s and 1930s were often difficult and dangerous. Emergency supplies and machine parts for remote mining or logging camps in the jungle or mountains often had to be flown in. Pilots had to land on tiny landing strips carved out of the jungle or mountainside.

In the south, air routes supplied remote towns such as Punta Arenas in southern Chile which is a thousand miles south of the nearest large town. Flying over the great empty plains of Patagonia in monoplanes, pilots often faced winds up to 80 mph, zero visibility, ice and snow. On the route between Santiago (Chile) and Buenos Aires (Argentina) planes flew over the 13,000-foot Uspallata pass between giant peaks such as Aconcagua and Tupungato.

Today, the airplane still provides isolated communities with a vital link to the outside world. Bolivia has more airfields than railroad stations. Advances in technology have made flying safer and more comfortable than it was in the early days.

*Los pioneros de los cielos (air pioneers) in South America flew in unpressurized planes. Flying over the Andes was dangerous, because flying above 12,000 feet requires the use of oxygen. Well-known pilots included Argentine aviator Vicente Almondos Almonacid, known as **el Cóndor de la Rioja**, and US pilot, Bob Reeve (above). Bob Reeve later went to Alaska where he was called the 'Glacier Pilot' because of his extraordinary ability to land on glaciers.*

¿Sabes que...?

★ In the 15th century, the Incas built a 15,000-mile road network. Many of the roads were paved with stones and can still be seen. In the mountains steps were cut into steep rock slopes. Rope bridges were suspended over canyons. There were no horses, so messages were carried by runners called **chasquis**. With this network, it took only six days for a message to travel from Quito to Cuzco, a distance of more than 950 miles. (Remember it took Christopher Columbus more than two months to sail across the Atlantic in 1492.)

★ The first person to fly over the Alps was Peruvian pilot Jorge Chávez. On September 23, 1910, in his fragile monoplane he reached an altitude of 7,250 feet as he flew over the Simplon Pass from Brig (Switzerland) to Domodossola (Italy). As Chávez landed, he was blown out of his plane and killed.

Before the Conquest

Antes de la llegada de los españoles en el continente suramericano había muchas culturas indígenas fascinadoras.

La leyenda de El Dorado

The Chibchas lived in the central highlands of Colombia in the area around the present-day capital of Bogotá. The king or chief, known as the **zipa**, inherited his position through his mother. Every new king underwent a special ceremony. He was covered in gold dust, and went to bathe in the sacred Lake Guatavita. At the same time the people threw gold objects into the lake.

This ceremony is thought to be the origin of the story of El Dorado, a legendary Amerindian king who ruled a land of fabulous wealth. The conquistadors heard the story on the Caribbean coast in 1509 and many expeditions were sent out to find El Dorado. When Jiménez de Quesada finally discovered Lake Guatavita in 1562, his men went fishing—for gold!

Several attempts were made to drain Lake Guatavita and find the gold objects that had been thrown in. The most serious attempt was made by Antonio de Sepúlveda in the 1580s. Eight thousand Indian workmen cut a great notch in the side of the lake to let the water run out. The water level was lowered 66 feet (20 meters) before the cut collapsed, killing many of the Indian workmen. Sepúlveda found a large quantity of gold objects and a huge emerald weighing 300 carats.

Since then, several attempts have been made to drain the lake and many gold ornaments recovered. In 1965, the Colombian government declared any attempts to plunder the lake illegal. Many thousands of gold objects can be seen in **el Museo de Oro** in Bogotá.

El lago de Guatavita, Colombia

Up to AD 1000, several pre-Columbian cultures—Paracas, Nazca, Chumú, Chancay and Mochica—flourished along the coast of Peru. They were largely peaceful and very talented at making pottery and weaving.

The Mochicas, who lived in the Moche Valley from AD 200 to 700, were very skilful potters. They made pots into portraits of nobles and commoners, and in the shape of animals, birds and plants.

Las líneas de Nazca

In southern Peru the desert is crisscrossed with hundreds of straight lines, geometric figures and giant animal drawings. Etched on the surface of the desert between 200 BC and AD 800, the Nazca Lines are on such a scale that they can only be seen properly from the air.

The lines were made by clearing away the darker oxidized surface stones. Because the climate is so dry and there is little wind, the lines have remained virtually unchanged for centuries. Even horse-hoof prints can be seen clearly for hundreds of years.

A German scientist, Maria Reiche, has spent more than 45 years in Peru studying the lines. They seem to have formed part of an astronomical calendar, possibly used to calculate when to plant crops. The increased number of visitors to the lines in recent times has caused problems. Some come by car and drive out across the desert to see the lines. The tire tracks now zigzag over the geometric figures and lines.

This map shows the names that have been given to the figures at Nazca.
- What animals or birds can you recognize from the drawings or from the Spanish names?
- Use a dictionary to find out the English equivalents of the words you don't know.

El imperio de los Incas

By the end of the 15th century the Inca empire stretched more than 2,000 miles (3,200 km) from what is now the Colombian-Ecuadorean border south to **el río Bio-Bio** in central Chile. East to west the Inca empire extended from the Peruvian coast into present-day Bolivia and northern Argentina. The empire was called **Tahuantinsuyo**, and it was divided into four regions with its center in Cuzco in the Andes.

Inca society was strictly organized. Everyone had to work and contribute to the common good; in return, the state supplied citizens with food, clothing and other necessities. In times of famine, food was distributed from state storehouses. There was no system of writing, but official records were kept on knotted strings called **quipus**.

People were liable for military service or public labor projects, like the construction of huge stone temples and buildings, and rows of stone terraces, **los andenes**. On **los andenes**, which were built up mountainsides, crops such as maize, potatoes and beans were cultivated. Elaborate irrigation systems with stone channels were constructed.

The Sapa Inca, the emperor, was thought to be semidivine. He had absolute power. Under him was a rigid hierarchy of priests and nobles. There were

El misterio del pasado

EL COLIBRI
LA ARAÑA
EL ALCATRAZ
LA IGUANA
EL CONDOR
EL ARBOL
EL LORO
EL MONO
EL PERRO
LAS MANOS
EL ASTRONAUTA
LA CARRETERA PANAMERICANA
LOS TRIANGULOS
LOS TRAPEZOIDES
NAZCA
LA BALLENA
RIO NAZCA
AEROPUERTO

La Conquista del Perú

Shortly before the Spaniards arrived in Peru, the Inca empire had been split by civil war. The northern part, with its capital in Quito, was ruled by Huáscar. The southern half, with its capital at Cuzco, was ruled by his half-brother Atahuallpa. Atahuallpa claimed the whole of the Inca empire for himself and killed Huáscar at the battle of Huancavelica in 1530.

When Francisco Pizarro and Diego de Almagro arrived on the coast in 1532, they took advantage of the situation. With his tiny force, Pizarro marched into the Andes to Cajamarca and took Atahuallpa prisoner. Pizarro promised Atahuallpa his freedom if he could fill a room in the palace with gold. The gold arrived, but in the end Atahuallpa was killed.

When Pizarro reached Cuzco, he was welcomed. But when **los conquistadores** plundered the city, the people saw the Spaniards were dangerous enemies and fought back. As in Mexico, horses and guns gave the Spaniards an initial advantage over the Inca soldiers. But the Inca warriors were tough and battle-hardened. In 1538, Manco Inca besieged Cuzco with an army and was beaten off only with difficulty.

Until his death in 1541, Pizarro gradually extended Spanish rule over the former Inca empire. In the 16th century the Spaniards explored and colonized other parts of South America. The local people continued to resist the take-over of their lands. In 1780, an Inca noble, Túpac Amaru, led an unsuccessful rebellion against the Spanish. In southern Chile and Argentina the Araucanian Indians fought against Spanish control until late in the 19th century.

Francisco Pizarro

Under Spanish rule, various books on Inca history were written. One historian was Felipe Guamán Poma de Ayala (c. 1526–1613) who claimed to be a descendant of a Sapa Inca. Guamán Poma's 1,200-page book El primer nueva corónica y buen gobierno (c. 1600) has 500 illustrations. Viracocha (below) was both an Inca emperor and a god. He taught humans useful skills, like the use of the taclla (foot-plough).

El Sapa Inca y su mujer, la coya

severe punishments for those who did not obey the law. Lawbreaking was considered as sacrilegious, because it was seen as disobedience to the semi-divine Sapa Inca.

The language of the Incas, Quechua, is still spoken by Indians living in the Peruvian Andes.

¿Sabes que...?

★ Some of the Inca terraces and irrigation systems are still in use.
★ In the Rafael Larco Herrera Museum in Lima, Peru, there is a piece of hand-woven pre-Columbian material that was woven so finely that it has 398 threads to the inch (156 to the centimeter)! Material for an average pair of blue jeans has approximately 65 threads per inch (26 per centimeter).

From colonies to nations

Las colonias de Nueva España

During the 16th and 17th centuries, while the territories of **Nueva España** were under Spanish rule, the Spanish tried to keep their New World colonies from trading with other countries. The colonies had to send their agricultural produce and minerals to Spain in exchange for goods and produce from **la madre patria**, Spain. The people in the colonies began to resent such controls, and English, Dutch and Portuguese ships took advantage of the situation to smuggle goods to the colonies of New Spain.

Smuggling later turned to piracy, as ships lay in wait to rob the Spanish treasure fleets. From bases in Jamaica and the Bahamas pirates also sailed to plunder coastal towns in the area.

Independence dates for Central and South American countries

Panamá 1903
Venezuela 1821
Guatemala 1821
Honduras 1821
El Salvador 1821
Nicaragua 1821
Costa Rica 1821
Colombia 1819
Ecuador 1822
Perú 1821
Bolivia 1825
Paraguay 1811
Chile 1818
Uruguay 1828
Argentina 1816

This map shows when the Spanish-speaking countries of Central and South America became independent. From 1821 to 1838 Guatemala, El Salvador, Honduras, Nicaragua and Costa Rica were part of a confederation called **las Provincias Unidas del Centro de América**.

Héroes de la independencia

At the time Mexico began to fight for independence, colonies in other parts of New Spain also demanded independence. Venezuelan revolutionary Simón Bolívar (1783–1830) became known as **el Libertador** for his crucial role in freeing South America from Spanish domination.

A separatist army led by Bolívar finally won freedom for Colombia at the battle of Boyacá in 1819. A second victory at the battle of Carabobo in 1821 secured independence for Venezuela. With Bolívar as president, the two areas, together with Ecuador, became **la República de Gran Colombia**.

In 1824, at the battles of Junín and Ayacucho, Bolívar and his general, Sucre, helped the Peruvians in the final defeat of the Spanish.

Simón Bolívar, el Libertador

Another great figure of South America's struggle for independence is José de San Martín (1778–1850). He was a professional soldier with the Spanish army in Europe. In 1812, he returned to his native Argentina to support the movement for independence. Argentina declared its independence in 1816.

In 1817, San Martín took command of an Argentine army which marched over the Andes to attack the Spanish armies in Chile and Peru. With Chilean eader Bernardo O'Higgins, he defeated the Spanish in the battles at Chacabuco and Maipú, and Chile became independent.

The last stronghold of Spanish power in South America was Peru. After three years of careful preparation, San Martín landed his troops in southern Peru in September, 1820. Although San Martín proclaimed Peru's independence in July, 1821, the Spanish forces did not leave.

In 1822, San Martín met Bolívar to ask his help in freeing Peru. What happened at the meeting in the port of Guayaquil (now in Ecuador) is not known, but afterwards San Martín returned to Argentina and then went into self-imposed exile in France, where he died in 1850. For his part in Peruvian independence, San Martín was called **el Protector del Perú**.

José de San Martín, el Protector del Perú

Chile's national hero is Bernardo O'Higgins (1778–1842) who ruled the country from independence in 1818 to 1823. Son of the Irish-born Viceroy of Peru Ambrose O'Higgins, Bernardo O'Higgins took part in a general revolt against the Spanish in 1810. By 1813, he had assumed command of Chile's revolutionary forces. After their defeat by the Spanish at the battle of Rancagua, O'Higgins and his remaining forces went to Argentina to seek help from San Martín.

It took San Martín three years to train the army. Bernardo O'Higgins accompanied San Martín as he marched the army over the rugged Andes, and defeated the Spanish. After independence San Martín was asked to become head of state, but he refused, and O'Higgins was appointed.

Bernardo O'Higgins

Ecuador became part of **la República de Gran Colombia** in 1822 when Bolívar sent his fellow Venezuelan, General Antonio José de Sucre (1795–1830), against the Spanish army in Ecuador. Marching north from Guayaquil, Sucre defeated the Spanish forces at a battle on the slopes of the volcano Pichincha, which overlooks Quito. Sucre's soldiers occupied Quito. The republic broke up in 1830, and Venezuela, Ecuador and Colombia became separate countries.

After helping defeat the Spanish at Ayacucho in Peru, Sucre attacked the Spanish armies in what is now Bolivia. In April, 1825, he won the battle of Tumusla, and the republic of Bolivia was established. Sucre was Bolivia's first president from 1826 to 1828.

● How do you think Bolivia got its name?

Antonio José de Sucre, el Mariscal de Ayacucho

¿Sabes que...?

★ When San Martín and Bolívar met in Guayaquil in 1822, they discussed the idea of a single South American state along the lines of the United States of America, but they could not agree on the form of government. San Martín wanted a monarchy and Bolívar, a republic.

CARACAS, LA CIUDAD NATAL DE BOLÍVAR

Casa Natal del Libertador: ubicada entre las esquinas de San Jacinto y Los Traposos, a una cuadra y media de la Plaza Mayor, o Plaza de Armas, que se conserva desde la Colonia y que hoy lleva el nombre del Héroe. Allí nació Simón Bolívar, el 24 de Julio de 1783. Es un museo histórico donde se pueden admirar numerosos objetos personales del Libertador.

La Plaza Bolívar: situada en lo que fue el corazón de la ciudad desde la época colonial, enmarcada por rectas calles, de acuerdo al clásico cuadriculado de las ciudades españolas. En su centro, rodeada por frondosos árboles, se levanta la estatua ecuestre de Bolívar, obra del escultor Tadolini.

Museo Bolivariano: contiguo a la casa natal, aquí se exhiben algunas pertenencias del Héroe, y de compañeros suyos durante la gesta emancipadora.

La Catedral: austera e imponente, guarda recuerdos históricos y religiosos de enorme valor. En ella fue bautizado Simón Bolívar y allí reposan los restos de sus padres y de su esposa.

This extract from a guidebook describes some of the places in Caracas, Venezuela, associated with Simón Bolívar.

● What is the date of Bolívar's birth?
● What memorial to Bolívar can be found in **la Plaza Bolívar**?
● What connection does **el Museo Bolivariano** have with the house where Bolívar was born?
● What happened to Bolívar in the cathedral?

¿Sabes que...?

★ Some of the currencies in Central and South America commemorate famous people:
   – **el bolívar** in Venezuela.
   – **el sucre** in Ecuador.

Los americanos

La gente de Centroamérica y de América del Sur viene de origen de países diversos.

Los inmigrantes

While vast areas of Latin America were under the Spanish control, only Spaniards were allowed to immigrate to the American colonies. After the South American countries became independent, up to nine million immigrants arrived between 1880 and 1930.

As well as from Spain and Portugal, immigrants came from many other European countries such as Italy, France, Germany, Britain, Switzerland, Greece and Yugoslavia. Even today, one in six Venezuelans was born abroad and about 13 per cent of Argentines are first-generation immigrants.

The different immigrant groups left their mark on the countries where they settled. In southern Patagonia in Argentina, there were Welsh settlements, including Trelew, Puerto Madryn, where Welsh, not Spanish, was the main language spoken. German immigrants founded towns like **Villa Alemana** (Chile) and **Alemania** (Argentina). The variety of surnames in a telephone directory from a country such as Chile, Peru or Venezuela gives an indication of the countries immigrants came from.

Not everyone came to the Spanish colonies as willing immigrants. Many thousands of people were taken from Africa and sent to Latin America to work as slaves, especially in the tropical areas. Today, their descendants live on the coasts of Venezuela, Colombia, Ecuador and Peru, and along the Central American Caribbean coast.

Americanas de descendencia africana

¿Cómo se llama?

Padre	Madre
Eduardo Flores B.	**María Rodríguez R.**

Full name: Roberto Flores Rodríguez

Shortened versions: Roberto Flores R.
Roberto Flores

*Every person has two surnames: one from the father and the other from the mother. For example, a man called **Roberto Flores Rodríguez** takes his father's surname, **Flores**, and his mother's maiden name, **Rodríguez**.*

Señorita Isabel Flores Rodríguez = Señor Carlos Castillo Aguilar

Señora Isabel Flores de Castillo

Shortened version: Señora Isabel Castillo

*When a woman marries, she keeps her father's surname and also takes her husband's surname. For example, if Roberto's sister, **Señorita Isabel Flores Rodríguez** marries **Señor Carlos Castillo Aguilar**, she will become **Señora Isabel Flores de Castillo**, or more simply, **Señora Isabel Castillo**.*

José Fernández Ballesteros

Susana Sadosky de Fernández

Humberto Rossi García

Yolanda Duarte de Rossi

tienen el gusto de participar a Ud. el próximo enlace de sus hijos

Luís Antonio y María Luisa

e invitarle a la ceremonia religiosa que se celebrará el día 3 de septiembre a las 18:00 horas, en el Templo de Santo Domingo, ubicado en Bolívar 45.

On this wedding invitation the names of the groom's parents appear above the names of the bride's parents.
- What was the maiden name of the groom's mother?
- What is the groom's full name?
- What will the bride's name be after her marriage?

¿De dónde viene?

Two people were asked to say something about the place they live in and some of the other places they have visited.

María Pasarella G.,
Buenos Aires, Argentina

❝ Yo soy porteña porque vivo en Buenos Aires, pero mi abuelo fue de origen italiano. Tengo 16 años y estudio en la secundaria.

Buenos Aires es una gran ciudad. En el centro hay muchos edificios antiguos como la Casa Rosada donde está la oficina del presidente, la catedral y el Teatro Colón.

En el verano paso las vacaciones con mi familia en Punta del Este en Uruguay. Vamos en avión. ❞

Osvaldo Mora Santacruz,
Otavalo, Ecuador

❝ Tengo 16 años y vivo en la ciudad de Otavalo que está cerca de Quito. Mi familia vive en esta región desde hace centenares de años.

Ahora trabajo, ayudando a mis padres. Ellos tejen vestidos y los venden en la Plaza de Ponchos en Otavalo. Hay muchos turistas extranjeros que vienen para comprar ponchos y blusas típicas.

Fui una vez a Quito para visitar a una tía que vive allá. No me gustó—era demasiado ruidoso. ❞

- What would you call a man who comes from Buenos Aires?
- Which country did María's grandfather come from?
- Has Osvaldo's family lived in the Otavalo area for a long time?
- Has Osvaldo ever visited Quito?
- Who is **el Teatro Colón** named after?

These signs are for businesses and organizations set up by people from different countries outside Latin America.
- From what country did the tea shop owner come?
- What other language might the hotel owner speak?
- What language, other than Spanish, would you expect to be taught at the school?
- Would you be likely to find spaghetti on the menu in the restaurant? Explain why.

Some schools were set up by different immigrant groups, so that children could learn about their parents' cultures. The schools usually teach the language of the immigrant group.
- Which two countries are mentioned here?
- What foreign languages are taught at the school?

¿Sabes que...?

★ It is useful to know both surnames when looking up someone in the phone book. There may be several pages of one name, if it is a common one. Within the name section, names will be listed alphabetically according to the second surname. For example, **Rodríguez Alvarez** will come before **Rodríguez Salas**.

★ In Argentina there are **periódicos** (newspapers) published in English, Italian, German and French. Peru has an English-language newspaper called *The Lima Times*.

El comercio exterior

El sector agropecuario

¿Cuáles son los productos en que comercian los países centroamericanos y sudamericanos?

Una plantación bananera

Bananas are grown in tropical areas throughout the world. Fray Tomás de Berlanga, a Spanish priest, is credited with introducing bananas to the Caribbean from Africa in 1516, although large-scale commercial cultivation of bananas in Central and South America began only in the late 19th century. In 1878, Costa Rica was the first Central American country to which bananas were introduced.

Together with coffee and sugar, bananas are major agricultural exports of many Central American countries. The USA is a big market, as most of its banana supply comes from Central America, Colombia and Ecuador.

Colombia is the second largest coffee producer in the world, Brazil being the first. Coffee accounts for about 20 percent of Colombia's total exports. Colombian coffee is a mild-flavored arabica coffee that can be picked all year round.

Colombia is **el país del café de montaña** because the best coffee grows at an altitude between 2,950 and 6,230 feet (900 and 1900 meters) above sea level in the Andes. Banana palms are often planted to give shade to young coffee trees, **cafetos**. Coffee beans are usually picked by hand because it is difficult to use machines in the mountains.

Most of the Central American countries also cultivate large quantities of coffee trees in highland areas.

Another important crop that grows well in the tropical areas of Central and South America is sugar cane. It was

La inspección del cafeto

introduced to the New World by Columbus in 1493.

When the cane is ready, it is cut and crushed to extract the sugary juice. The liquid is refined into sugar crystals and other products. The residue that is left after crushing is used as fuel, animal fodder, or in paper making.

Cuba has traditionally been the world's largest exporter, and the second largest producer, of sugar. A recent bad harvest forced Cuba to suspend many of its exports.

The flat plains of Argentina and Uruguay, **la pampa**, provide excellent grazing for cattle. The cowboy of the

Un gaucho en un rodeo de ganado

pampa, **el gaucho**, is famous for his riding skills and ability to withstand the hard and lonely life of the plains. Since colonial times, leather and leather goods have been exported from this area. With the advent of refrigeration at the end of the 19th century, the mass export of beef began.

Vast areas of the pampas are also given over to arable farming, mainly cereal growing. Argentina is the fourth largest exporter of soybeans in the world.

Peru and Chile look to the sea for one major export— fish and fishmeal products. The cold Humboldt current contains large stocks of fish, especially anchovies, but overfishing in recent years has reduced the fish stocks.

Periodically, as happened in 1992, a warm water current called **el Niño** appears and drives away most of the fish. Later, it disappeared again and fish catches have improved.

¡Mira!

☞ Look at the bananas that you see on sale in the US. Which countries do they come from?

☞ What country does your favorite coffee come from?

★ Potatoes, **las papas**, originate in the Andes, where they grow at altitudes of up to 14,000 feet (4,267 meters) above sea level. They were first taken from South America back to Europe by the Spaniards in the 16th century.

    The Incas used to freeze-dry potatoes (**chuño**). They left potatoes out to freeze overnight and then to thaw and dry out in the sun. People in the Andes still make **chuño** in the traditional way.

★ Corn is cultivated as a staple food throughout Central and South America. It can grow at altitudes of up to 10,000 feet (3,048 meters) above sea level.

    It is used in many different ways: in bread, in soup, in chicken pie, and even in maize beer.

This gum from Peru has a special flavor. **Chicha morada** is a non-alcoholic drink made from purple corn, with fruit and sugar added. Purple corn is also used to make a dessert called **mazamorra morada**.

● How do you say 'chewing gum' in Spanish?

La exportación minera

Several South American countries are now oil exporters. The first oil discovered in Venezuela was found near Lake Maracaibo in 1914. Venezuela obtains nearly 80 percent of its export income from oil. Ecuador is dependent on oil exports for 37 percent of its foreign earnings. Bolivia is a major exporter of natural gas.

    Oil deposits are often in remote areas. Peru's main oil reserves are in the jungle near the border with Ecuador, Colombia and Brazil. In both Peru and Ecuador there are **oleoductos** (pipelines) which carry oil from jungle areas up over the mountains and down to the coast for export. In Colombia, **oleoductos** carry oil from **los llanos**, the eastern plains, to the coast.

    Thirty percent of Argentina's oil production comes from the bleak, windswept Patagonian plains around Comodoro Rivadavia. **Un gasoducto** (gas pipeline) carries natural gas 1,100 miles north to Buenos Aires.

The largest open-cast mine in the world is Chuquicamata in Chile. Excavations began there in 1915 and the mine is now 1,860 feet deep. The depression is so large that it can be detected from the moon. Chile is the world's largest copper producer, with a quarter of the world's known reserves.

*A land drilling rig in **los llanos** of eastern Colombia.*

*The Spanish found silver at **el Cerro Rico** in Bolivia in 1545. At the foot of the mountain they built the town of Potosí. By the end of the century Potosí had a population of 150,000 and had become the world's richest city. The expression **vale un Potosí** is still used to describe anything extremely valuable. Today, the silver is gone, but small amounts of tin and other metals are still mined at Cerro Rico. Tin accounts for 20 percent of Bolivia's overseas earnings.*

Sitios turísticos

¿Visitemos algunos sitios turísticos?

El patrimonio inca

Although the Spaniards pulled down many Inca palaces and temples and built their churches and public buildings on top, Inca stonework can still be seen in the streets of Cuzco.

La calle Loreto is a street with the stone walls of Inca palaces down each side. In Inca times, it was called **Inti Kicllu** or Sun Street.

Around the city there are also many Inca ruins. On a hill above Cuzco stands the ruined fort of Sacsayhuamán. It had three sets of walls, built in a zigzag shape. Some of the huge boulders at the base of the walls weigh up to 300 tons (300 tonnes); one rock is nearly 30 feet (9 meters) high.

At the winter solstice in June, the Festival of the Sun, Inti Raymi, is held at Sacsayhuamán. Local people dress in pre-Columbian costumes and there are ceremonial processions and dances.

¿Sabes que...?

★ In **la calle Hatunrumiyoq** in Cuzco is the Palace of Inca Roqa. The wall of the palace is made of stone blocks. One large block has 12 angles, each of which fits into another surrounding block. In Quechua, **hatun** means 'big' and **rumi** 'stone'.

MONUMENTOS PRE COLOMBINOS

AJLLA WASI.— Casa de las Vírgenes del Sol, en la calle Loreto.
PALACIO DE QOLQANPATA.— Supuestamente Palacio de Manco Qhapaq y de Paullo Inca, sito en la Parroquia de San Cristobal.
AMARU CANCHA.— Palacio de Huayna Qhapaq, área actualmente ocupada por la Iglesia de la Compañía de Jesús.
QORA QORA.— Palacio de Sinchi Roca, área ocupada por el Portal de Carnes e inmuebles contiguos.
QASANA.— Palacio de Pachacuteq, área ocupada por el Portal de Panes y casas aledañas.
HATUN CANCHA.— Palacio de Tupac Inca Yupanki, área ocupada por el Portal de Belén, y edificios contiguos a la calle Triunfo.
PUCA MARCA.— Área comprendida entre las calles San Agustín, Maruri y Arequipa.
QORICANCHA.— Templo del Sol, área ocupada por la Iglesia y Convento de Santo Domingo.
KISWAR CANCHA.— Palacio de Wiraqocha, área que ocupa la Basílica Catedral.
HATUNRUMIYOQ.— Palacio de Inca Roqa, donde se encuentra la famosa piedra de los doce ángulos, en la calle del mismo nombre.

This extract lists Inca sites in Cuzco. Some of the buildings have disappeared completely.

The Quechua names for the sites are also given. The Quechua words may look strange, because they are written to represent Quechua sounds, some of which may not exist in Spanish pronunciation or spelling. The Quechua 'll' is pronounced as an 'l' sound, so the name of the Inca emperor Atahuallpa is written with 'll'.

● What other way of spelling 'Wiraqocha' have you seen in this book?
● What building was constructed on top of the Temple of the Sun?

The Inca city of Machu Picchu in Peru was built on a mountain top 8,038 feet (2,450 meters) above sea level. Until it was found in 1911 by Professor Hiram Bingham of Yale University, the city had lain overgrown by jungle for hundreds of years. Today, Machu Picchu can be reached by train from Cuzco, 70 miles (112 km) away. In Inca times, the city was linked to the Inca capital by a road, parts of which can still be seen.

The whole city is built of massive granite blocks which were cut and shaped without the use of iron tools. Walls were built without cement and the blocks fit together so tightly that a knife blade cannot be pushed between them. The walls have withstood several earthquakes.

The reason for building a city here is uncertain, but it was probably a religious center. On the site there are temples, a lookout tower and houses. Below the city were constructed a series of **andenes**, terraces, to grow food for the inhabitants.

The Peruvian Andes are dotted with the remains of many Inca buildings. There may still be undiscovered 'lost cities'.

Sol y nieve

Every year from December to mid-April (summer-time in the southern hemisphere) up to a million tourists from Argentina and Brazil go to Uruguay to enjoy its beaches. Along the estuary of **el río de la Plata**, the beaches stretch in an unbroken chain from the capital, Montevideo, to the Atlantic Ocean at Punta del Este.

The narrow peninsula of Punta del Este is the largest and best known of the resorts along the 199-mile (320-km) Uruguayan coastline. On the bay side is **la playa mansa** for those who like a quiet swim. For those who like rougher water or surfing, there is **la playa brava**, the beach on the Atlantic Ocean side.

Winter sports fans head down to southern Chile and Argentina for the ski season which runs from July to September. Just over 1,000 miles (1,600 km) south of Buenos Aires is the ski resort of San Carlos de Bariloche in Argentina's Lake District. The town is set between the foot of **el Cerro Otto** and the shores of **el lago Nahuel Huapí** in **el Parque Nacional de los Glaciares**. A cable car and chairlift system carries skiers up to **las pistas de esquí** (the ski runs) at **el Cerro Catedral**.

The ski resort is also a good center for exploring the rest of the national park. The spectacular landscape of snow-capped mountains and glacial lakes attracts walkers, mountain climbers and fishermen.

In the Chilean Andes, there are several popular winter sports centers, including Portillo, La Parva, El Colorado and Valle Nevado. All are close to the capital, Santiago.

This ad is offering ski holidays.

- What is unusual about the word 'ski' which appears in this ad?
- In which country are the ski resorts?
- What is the slogan for the airline which is organizing the tours?

¿Sabes que...?

★ The highest ski run in the world is in Bolivia. Chacaltaya, near La Paz, has a rope tow up to 17,129 feet (5,221 meters).

La pista de esquí de Chacaltaya

Carnaval en...Oruro

Carnivals are held all over Latin America. They developed from religious ceremonies that marked the beginning of Lent, a period of austerity leading up to Easter.

One famous carnival, **la Diablada**, takes place at Oruro, a mining town high in the Bolivian Andes. The origins of **la Diablada** lie in the Conquest, when the Indians were forced to work in the mines. As an outlet for their hardships, the Indians danced the legend of the invasion of Earth by Hell's evil powers and the final triumph of good over evil. Christian elements were later introduced, with the Devil representing evil and St. Michael the Archangel representing good. The ceremony is dedicated to **la Virgen de Socavón**, the madonna of the mine.

During the eight-day carnival, as well as watching the dancers, spectators enjoy themselves by throwing **globos** or **bombas de agua** (small balloons filled with water), or firing water pistols at each other.

*A leaflet for **la Diablada** showing the dancers wearing typical devil masks.*

Time off

El ritmo latino

Salsa dance music is a kind of musical melting pot, including original Indian music, the use of instruments introduced by the Spanish such as the guitar and the trumpet, and drums, percussion and complex rhythms from Africa.

The roots of **la salsa** lie in Cuba, but it also encompasses traditional dance music from the Dominican Republic, Puerto Rico, Colombia and Venezuela. **Salsa** appeared in Cuba in the 1920s. Later, in the 1930s, many Cuban musicians settled in New York, where they began to play **salsa** with other Latin American and jazz musicians.

These albums are by two different generations of salsa music makers:
- Celia Cruz (singer) and Johnny Pacheco (pianist)
- Rubén Blades (singer/songwriter)

At play

> A la gente de América Latina le apasiona el futbol.

El futbol has always roused passionate feelings in Latin America. In 1969 there was the 'Soccer War' between El Salvador and Honduras. Although the real cause of the war was illegal Salvadorean immigration into Honduras, hostilities broke out after El Salvador beat Honduras 3–2 in a World Cup soccer match.

The South American nations of Brazil, Argentina and Uruguay have won eight of the 15 World Cup competitions held. Uruguay won the very first World Cup in 1930. Famous soccer players are treated like national heroes.

Every year, South America holds its own special soccer competition called **la Copa Libertadores de América** which started in 1960. Teams from Argentina, including Independiente, River Plate and Boca Juniors, have won **la Copa Libertadores** many times. Uruguayan teams, such as Peñarol and Nacional Montevideo, also have a good record in this competition. A less well-known cup winner is Olimpia of Paraguay which has won twice.

TV DEPORTES

Caracol está transmitiendo los partidos de la Copa Libertadores de América, el evento futbolístico más importante del continente suramericano.

Los televidentes, por primera vez podrán disfrutar no sólo los encuentros del Grupo A en donde estaremos representados por el América de Cali, sino también los del Grupo B que en esta oportunidad se caracteriza por contar con los equipos más importantes de Argentina y Uruguay, entre ellos el River Plate (Buenos Aires).

Read this TV information about **la Copa Libertadores** from a Colombian magazine.
- What is the Spanish word for 'television viewers'?
- Which team is representing Colombia in Group A?
- Which two countries have teams in Group B?